Verbs as Guidance

A Guide for the Leader Within

Verbs as Guidance: A Guide for the Leader Within

Laura Newberry-Yokley

Sonrisa
PRODUCTS

Wooster, Ohio, USA © 2021

Verbs as Guidance: A Guide for the Leader Within
Written by: Laura Newberry-Yokley

Published by:
Sonrisa Products LLC
1527 Willoughby Drive
Wooster, OH 44691 USA
001-614-202-2198
SonrisaProducts.com

ISBN: 978-0-578-89398-3
Cover Art: Corey Hosfeld
Copyeditor: Joella Good Newberry

For additional copies, contact Sonrisa Products LLC at
+1 614-202-2198, estrotar@gmail.com, or visit
SonrisaProducts.com.

Printed in the United States of America.

"Guidance comes easier when viewed as a verb rather than a noun."

-Carolyn Myss, PhD

"Action is the foundational key to all success."

-Pablo Picasso

"Take the action and the insight follows."

-Anne Lamont

Other Books by Laura Newberry-Yokley

Lights Out at Midnight by Evangelist Beverly Yokley & Laura Newberry-Yokley

Christian Healing 365: A Daily Devotional Reader

Healing Calendar 365: A Holistic Leadership Tool

Author's Note

What are verbs?
Verbs are action words.

What is action?
Action is the Sanskrit word called *karma*, or the spiritual principle of cause and effect, reaping and sowing. More distinctly, *karma* is the energy created by a person's actions that determines consequences and outcomes.

Why are actions important?
Actions bring thoughts and emotions into existence, thereby creating habits. Actions shift our realities. Even a small drop of water can dissolve a boulder. We have the power to change our *karma* and create the futures we want.

A Special Consideration for Our Time:
This book was originally written in 2015, but it was never published. In 2020, a global pandemic caused the world to quarantine and halt its social and economic

practices. Many souls left. Many more were affected personally by COVID-19. Reality, as we knew it, ceased to exist. The illusion of certainty vanished. No longer could busy-ness shroud difficulty. No longer could we numb our feelings. Life fundamentally changed. It is as if, in the alchemy of life, we were boiled alive. As base metal, our impurities were brought to the surface. It is the hope that we emerge as the gold we were meant to be. We have been called to rebuild a new reality, brick by brick. May this guide help foster actions that bring about positive changes. As we learn to do things differently, may we be our own best guides.

Leadership is about fully knowing who you are so you can help others be fully who they are. *Verbs as Guidance* is a leadership guide geared to meet two goals:

(1.)   To conduct a full self-examination.

(2.)   To help you consistently do what you say you will do.

Nobody else but you is equipped to tell you what is going on inside your head, heart, body, and spirit. That is why you are the best leader for the job. Leadership is essentially the practice of open and honest self-awareness. Modeling the way, you can encourage others to do the same.

If you can practice being there for yourself, then you can be there with others and for others. At its basic level, leadership is about follow-through. People will be looking to you for that consistency, so do what you say you will do. It will change your life.

Assigning action items as inner guidance, and doing them, will help you build awareness of yourself and the outside world. Not only will it burst through your emotional clutter, but also it will improve your authenticity as a leader. This process will help you move through blockages. It is time to clean up unfinished business. Through the law of attraction, you will be able to create more good.

With each chapter, you may be wondering, "Why these words?" These verbs (action words) have been carefully selected as guidance designed to help you deepen and open. Now is an important time to guide yourself with patience and grace.

Originally, this book was developed as a leadership series that was to be comprised of four parts: Be, Rise, Lead, and Flow. Each book was to include 13 action words to assist you in rounding out your understanding of yourself and your leadership style. Five years later, I have updated the series to be one comprehensive, easy-to-use guide that includes these four parts, but in easy-to-use alphabetical order.

As I've already mentioned, you are your own best guide. Allow your insights to lead the way. As you unfold who you really are on a deeper level, you can do this difficult work. This work is as encouraging as it is challenging. Each action word contains an explanation, as well as space for you to talk, listen, journal, and draw, thereby creating your own guidance, right inside this book. This process requires a great deal of patience and compassion. You can purposefully position your actions, thoughts, and feelings in such a way that you can begin to move forward—differently. Choose to do so. You get to move forward. You get to heal. You get to lead.

To access your whole being, use all the tools you have:

• Speak – Ask yourself questions. The answers are already built into them. Read them in the spaces between each word.

• Listen – Check in with your heart. Be silent and let it speak. Your inner voice might not speak up at first. Be patient as you allow yourself to emerge.

• Write – Write down words, thoughts, whatever comes to mind. Just let them come. Do not worry about spelling everything right or using perfect grammar. It's actually better if you don't control the process. Just flow.

- Draw – Even if you "don't draw," let your visual, creative side express itself. Sometimes switching hands and drawing with your less dominant hand will help your spirit emerge from behind your ego.

Thank you for investing in yourself.

Table of Contents

1 Absorb.

To absorb means to take in energy through some sort of activity or thought. The challenge here is that you will take in both positive and negative energy. How do you decide which to accept into your atmosphere? What do you allow? If you are super empathic, absorbing might cause you difficulty. You might take on others' emotions as your own. Discernment will be crucial here. You will need to keep a keen eye, as your own ever-loving observer and protector, to know what will harm or help you.

There is a wonderful Tibetan Buddhist practice called Tonglen. "Tong" means giving and "Len" means taking. This practice is known as mixing self and other, sending and receiving at the same time. (1.) Take in pain; (2.) Send out relief. Even as you open up wide, take it all in, and send out big love to others and to the world. The world needs this practice now more than ever. As you pray for things and/or experiences to come into your life, count your blessings, and say thank you for all of the many wonderful things that have shown up. Pema Chödrön has great readings on this topic.

Absorbing, or being absorbed in something, can also mean having a great deal of attention. Are you able to read a book on your favorite subject for hours? Perhaps you are an artist, say great at stained glass or awesome at sewing. These activities bring you great joy, and you are able to spend hours on your projects without realizing it. Find what you are passionate about, and focus your attention there. You will find that the more you focus on something, the more it comes into your life.

Affirmation: Today I will remain watchful for what I bring into my emotional stratosphere. I am safe to give out good vibes, or relief, and I am willing to receive all the world has to offer, including pain and suffering. I am ready to absorb.

Speak about ABSORBING.

Allow the questions to come. What will it take to both send and receive love? What do I absorb? How do I know? What can I do to protect myself from anything negative I bring into my emotional atmosphere? Here are five (or more) questions that I ask about absorption.

(1.) _____

(2.) _____

(3.) _____

(4.) _____

(5.) _____

Listen. What messages emerge?

What other messages do I hold or receive about absorbing? What are my next best right steps?

Create a list of things you would like to give and receive.

?

?

?

?

?

?

?

Write about ABSORPTION.

Write about what you enjoy doing. What makes you excited? What brings you great joy? What do you do, spend hours doing it, and do not realize that so much time has passed? How can you spend more time doing these activities? Have you tried the *Tonglen* practice? If so, did it increase your level of compassion?

_____

_____

_____

_____

_____

_____

_____

_____

_____

_____

_____

_____

_____

_____

Draw ABSORB. What are you taking in? What are you sending out?

2 Accept.

To accept means to agree, to welcome, to acquire. The act of welcoming yourself into your own life is a wonderful concept of self-welcoming and self-love. Perhaps the most important part of self-acceptance is to become friends with your own company. Often one of the most difficult things to learn is self-acceptance and self-appreciation. It is right up there with radical forgiveness, especially when directed at ourselves.

The act of accepting does not mean that you put up with stuff or experiences that are toxic to your body, mind, spirit, or soul. That is not allowed. If something is not right, fix it immediately or remove yourself from the situation. If you decide to accept a situation, then you actively give yourself permission to participate in staying put and staying present. You are never stuck! You GET TO be part of a situation. What will you bring to the table? How will you show up? How will you make it better?

Imagine welcoming into your life a new level of abundance that you haven't had before, or a sense of satisfaction that you haven't experienced yet. Before you are able to do this, though, you will need to appreciate and accept all that is around and within you.

Acceptance is the act of receiving. When someone gives you something, you say, "thank you." Acceptance arrives with a certain level of gratitude. "Thank you," you can say. "Thank you for showing up in my life. What do you have to teach me?"

A sense of willingness often accompanies acceptance. Willingness brings about a feeling of readiness. Are you ready to bring love and abundance into your life? Are you ready to have positive outcomes show up in your life? Are you ready?

Affirmation: I am ready to receive. I am grateful for all that has shown up in my life. I am safe to accept simultaneously the situation as it is, and as I would like it to be.

Speak about ACCEPTANCE.

Allow the questions to come. What will it take to be in love with my life? Here are five (or more) questions that I have about radical acceptance.

(1.) _____

(2.) _____

(3.) _____

(4.) _____

(5.) _____

Listen. What messages emerge?

What other messages do I have about acceptance, willingness, receiving, and gratitude? What are my next best right steps?

Create a list of more verbs to help you move forward with abundance.

?

?

?

?

?

?

?

Write about ACCEPTANCE.

Notice the sounds, light, and temperature around you. Start there with your physical surroundings. Take note; now welcome these conditions into your heart. Become comfortable with them. Now, go inside. What do you notice? Notice your thoughts, emotions, and fears. Write down everything you notice (nothing is neither good nor bad, as Shakespeare has written, but thinking makes it so). Now, welcome these feelings, thoughts, and fears, into your heart. Appreciate that they are there for whatever purpose or lesson they may serve in your life.

_____

_____

_____

_____

_____

_____

_____

_____

Draw ACCEPT. How does it show up?

3 Act.

The good news is that taking action happens by doing something. The goal here is to act on purpose. Your actions can actually be a spiritual practice. The word Karma means action, work, or deed. Karma is the spiritual principle of cause and effect. What are your intentions? They are just as important as the actions themselves.

Do something. Anything. Taking action is akin to making movement happen. Move! Get up! Get going! We must move. We must take action. Actions are connected to your emotions and thoughts. If your body stops moving, so do your ideas and feelings. We must keep things flowing on all fronts. See FLOW for more.

To act also means to put on a show or have a pretense. It will be important for you to examine the dramatic role you play as the star of your life. What role do you play? Who are the supporting actors? It will also be important for you to check in to see if you are acting with authenticity or "putting on an act."

As a leader, your team will be looking to you for direction and guidance. They most certainly will be listening to your words in relation to your actions. They will be watching you very closely to see what you actually do. Did you do what you said you would do? Matching your words and actions brings about integrity. Did you follow through? Follow-through brings about consistency. Are you willing to do everything that you ask others to do? Demonstrating dignity for all and showing that all work is honorable brings about trust and respect. Eliminate your double standards.

Affirmation: I will make sure that I keep moving forward, whether or not my action is a very small one. I will get moving! I will check in to make sure I am coming from an authentic place. I will make sure my words match my deeds. I will create trust with my team by putting their needs first.

Speak about taking ACTION.

Allow the questions to come. What will it take to create more action in my life? Here are five (or more) questions that I ask about creating integrity through my actions.

(1.) _____

(2.) _____

(3.) _____

(4.) _____

(5.) _____

Listen. What messages emerge?

What other messages do I now realize about spiritual action, integrity, honoring all work, and increasing trust through my deeds?

?

?

?

?

?

?

?

?

?

Write about ACTING up or out.

Are you acting up? Are you putting on an act? Are you covering up? Are you acting from personality or a false ego-self? From your core spirit-self? Are you hiding? Check in here to make sure that you are being yourself and acting from a place of sincerity and honesty. Believe it or not, others can always tell if you're being real with them or using pretense.

_____

_____

_____

_____

_____

_____

_____

_____

_____

_____

_____

_____

_____

_____

Draw ACT. what does it look like?

4 Affect.

People often get confused here. "Affect" with an "a" is the verb that means to have an effect on or make a difference to. "Effect" with an "e" is the noun, or the result that happens when you "affect" it. Effect can also be a verb. It means to cause or bring about something. Affect has to do with creating change and impact. To affect something means to create impact or to make a difference. Someone can also be moved emotionally when they are affected by something.

Understanding what causes something will help you be able to push effects into motion. For example, many people procrastinate for many reasons but it's usually not because they just don't feel like doing something. Sometimes worthiness and self-esteem issues are wrapped into the procrastination. Get to the bottom of it. How about emotional eating or chronic tardiness? What's the root cause for these? Once you know the causes, then you can begin to affect the outcomes. You won't be as successful if you start with the undesired effects themselves. Get to the root of what's causing them in the first place.

So how do you affect the world around you? Do not be concerned if the effects that you create are small in nature. Small things grow into big things. Make sure you express gratitude for all you are able to put into motion, for all the effects you are able to cause. Creating change might happen gradually over time. Start to affect your surroundings in positive ways. Do you volunteer your time at a local non-profit? Do you clean up trash along your walking path? Find even the smallest activity and start there. The effects will soon become visible.

Affirmation: I will spend some time deciding how I want to affect my inner and outer worlds. I will think deeply about the root causes of the effects I desire create. I will work to create change, no matter how small it is. I will just start.

Speak about AFFECT.

Allow the questions to come. What does it mean to create effect, or affect and effect change? Here are five (or more) questions that I ask about affecting myself and others.

(1.) _____

(2.) _____

(3.) _____

(4.) _____

(5.) _____

Listen. What messages emerge?

What other messages do I have about cause and effect? What messages emerge about affecting positive outcomes around me? How might I be a change agent to bring about powerful impact?

?

?

?

?

?

?

?

?

Write about AFFECT, creating effects.

Cause and effect don't just happen in a vacuum. You actually have a great deal of control over what you think, about how your emotions show up, and what you do about them. Write about several effects that you would like to see in your life and in the world around you. What are their causes? What do you need to do in order to bring them to fruition?

_____

_____

_____

_____

_____

_____

_____

_____

_____

_____

_____

_____

_____

Draw AFFECT. what do its effects look like?

5 Aspire.

To aspire means to direct your attention and focus towards achieving something. Aspiration has a lot to do with ambition. Being ambitious includes being determined and hard-working. It is not just about hard work and determination, though. To aspire means that you focus on something specific, and then you work hard to get to that specific goal, whatever it is.

The best advice I've ever received was this: We always get what we ask for, and it may come as the reason we need. Once we ask, we need to allow. This means focusing on the thing that we've asked for, so that it will appear in physical form. If we focus on something else, that is what will be brought into focus, and therefore will be manifested. Aspire, then allow, then focus. The law of attraction will bring it to you!

Aspiration has everything to do with achieving. Achieving is a strong desire to do or obtain something. It typically requires determination or hard work. It is important to remember that this doesn't just suddenly happen. It happens during small moments, over a period of time.

Practice makes progress. It isn't about being perfect. Trying to be a better version of your best self is the name of the game. If you can do one thing differently today that will make a change, and repeat tomorrow, then you will start to see a difference. The key is to start. Beginning is 90% of the challenge, and the last 10% keeps the party going.

Affirmation: I will speak into being my aspiration. It is okay to work hard for what I want and expect to get it. I deserve what I ask for. I will receive what I aspire to. Opening my arms up to possibility, I allow newness to come into my life.

Speak about ASPIRE.

Allow the questions to come. What does it mean to ask for what I want and get it? Here are five (or more) questions that I ask about my goals, ambitions, and aspirations.

(1.) _____

(2.) _____

(3.) _____

(4.) _____

(5.) _____

Listen. What messages emerge?

What other messages do I have about my ambitions and my aspirations? What blockages do I have about my aspirations? Once I write them down, they will no longer hold me captive, and I will be able to move past them.

Say them aloud, and push through your fear. You will receive everything you ask for, everything you need.

?

?

?

?

?

?

Write about APSIRING, putting what you want out there.

Write down what your heart desires. Imagine your future self. What will he, she, or they be doing? What would you like them to be creating? Don't judge your answers. Without judgement, you will be able to ask for what you want...and get it. Put your desires into the vortex. You always get what you ask for. You always get what you need. (Editor's Note: I can think of so many situations that don't come to fruition: illness, death, poverty...write these down here, too.)

_____

_____

_____

_____

_____

Draw ASPIRE. what does your aspiration look like?

6 Assist.

To assist means to help. I am immediately reminded of Mr. Rogers when he said, "When I was a boy and I would see scary things in the news, my mother would say to me, 'Look for the helpers. You will always find people who are helping.'" Find the people who are helping, even when it is inconvenient for them to do so. The very essence of leadership is helping.

Here are some things you can do to assist:
- Return a favor.
- Do something unsolicited.
- Pay for someone's coffee or meal.
- Make an impact.
- Include everyone in the conversation.
- Be loving.
- Make the world a better place.
- Trust your team.

Affirmation: I will do my very best to assist wherever I am needed. I will give freely and with gratitude for the opportunity to do so. I will look for the helpers, I will surround myself with them, and I will commit to becoming a helper. I will help make positive changes in my own life and in the world around me. I will practice radical forgiveness, keep gratitude as the best attitude, and choose peacefulness in a world of chaos. I will help others to do the same. I will be kind. I will give grace.

Speak about ASSIST.

Allow the questions to come. What does it mean to assist, to help? Here are five (or more) questions that I ask about offering, asking for, and accepting assistance.

(1.) _____

(2.) _____

(3.) _____

(4.) _____

(5.) _____

Listen. What messages emerge?

What other messages do I have about assistance? What messages emerge about offering to help? Are there ever experiences when assistance is not required or wise? Rule of thumb, helping is a sister-cousin to enabling and potentially to co-dependency. If someone can do something for themselves on their own, assistance may not be needed. Find a meaningful space where your help would be encouraged. Never offer help as a form of control. This action must be given freely with no strings attached.

?

?

?

?

Write about ASSISTING, helping each other.

It was a snowy day. I got out of my car and was preparing to walk across the icy parking lot. A woman, who had difficulty walking, also got out of her car. I stopped and asked her if I could hold her hand. She was so thankful, and so was I. We walked across the parking lot together laughing and talking the entire way. How do you help others? More importantly, do you access aid when it is extended to you? Do you know how to ask for help?

_____
_____
_____
_____
_____
_____
_____
_____

Draw ASSISTING others or the world around you. Perhaps you might also draw asking for help or accepting others' help.

7 Awaken.

One of the most beautiful human beings I have ever met was babysitting my children. We were talking about "being woke" and she said to me, "Laura, even woke people have to keep waking up." Enlightenment happens in every moment of every day. We must continue to deepen, continue to wake up.

Our manifestations are ours alone for the purpose of shedding trauma and healing ourselves from real or perceived damage. We must continue to grow, to deepen, to find ourselves, and to fall madly in love with ourselves. Without this, we only hover above the surface of our lives.

Awaken to your intuition, to your inner guidance. Allow yourself to show yourself the way. Your inner guide will show you how to wake up. For most people, it's a slow, deliberate process. However, sometimes epiphanies will arise and take you by surprise. Both are wonderful.
I think of Buddha's enlightenment. He had

wandered for years, struggling and enduring many difficulties. Despite the difficulty, he was able to find "the middle path." At the end, seated just beneath a Bodhi tree, the demon, Mara, tried to seduce him with images of beautiful women. Do not be distracted. Siddhartha, or the Buddha, drank milk right before achieving enlightenment. You must exist in the world and you must love yourself enough to nourish your body and your dreams. Don't forget. Waking up includes these things.

Affirmation: As many times as I have awakened in my lifetime, I will continue to wake up. I will watch as the phoenix rises from the ashes. May the many distractions in my life not govern my attention. Might I focus on healing myself, others around me, and the world. Might I hold each moment dear, for that is all we really have!

Speak about being AWAKE.

Allow the questions to come. Am I asleep? Am I dreaming? Here are five (or more) questions that I ask about my own enlightenment, about my own constant state of waking up.

(1.) _____

(2.) _____

(3.) _____

(4.) _____

(5.) _____

Listen. What messages emerge?

What questions do I have about waking up? What does it feel like? How will I know when it happens? How can I be the co-creator in my awakening? How might I live my life in a constant state of waking up, of healing? If I could spend the rest of my life healing, wouldn't that be something?

?

?

?

?

?

?

?

Write AWAKENING into being.

A dear friend reminded me to focus on the donut and not the hole. What is keeping you asleep? How might you document it here in order to move it out of the way? Waking up happens in each moment of every day. Express what your waking up feels like to you.

_____

_____

_____

_____

_____

_____

_____

_____

_____

_____

_____

_____

_____

_____

_____

_____

Draw your AWAKENING. what does waking up look like?

8 Be.

As Ram Dass has written, you've likely heard the suggestion, "Be here now." This is the present moment reminding you to stay put. Living in the present moment helps keep you sane and healthy, as opposed to becoming overwhelmed and unhealthy.

I know your brain understands what I said, but do you really know how to just be? Imagine that you are sitting in a room by yourself. What do you do? Most of us would get our phones out and go through emails or mindlessly scroll through our social feeds. What would you be thinking about? Most of us would be lost in thought, either remembering what happened yesterday or anticipating tomorrow's events that are yet to come. What would you be feeling? Most likely, you might feel a bit of anxiety. Nobody really likes being with themselves without outside distractions.

Our shadow side scares us. Mostly we are afraid of what we already know about our shortcomings or fears. Oddly enough, we don't know the extent to which our power and strength sustains us and keeps us alive and well. That's what makes us go off and leave the present moment—our power. Where's your spirit in this moment? Your spirit IS. Beyond your actions, thoughts, and feelings lies something greater. Presence is when you commune with your spirit. What does that mean? When you allow yourself to witness yourself beyond what you're thinking about, what you're doing, and how you're feeling, therein lies your "being-ness." It might feel a bit like "nothing-ness."

Affirmation: I am that I am that I am. I am. I am me. I am here. I am safe.

Speak about your essential IS-NESS.

Allow the questions to come. Who am I? Here are five (or more) questions that I ask about my being and how I show up in my life.

(1.) _____

(2.) _____

(3.) _____

(4.) _____

(5.) _____

Listen. What messages emerge?

What other messages do I have about being-ness? What are my next best right steps? How do I put into action things that sustain my core being?

?

?

?

?

?

?

?

?

?

Write IS-NESS into being.

You are your own best guide. Allow your insights to lead the way as you unfold who you really are on a deeper level. You can purposefully position your actions, thoughts, and feelings in such a way that you can begin to move forward. Ask yourself, "What is missing in this present moment?" Just allow the answer to come. I think you'll find that nothing is missing.

_____
_____
_____
_____
_____
_____
_____
_____
_____
_____
_____
_____
_____

Draw BEING-NESS.
Repeat the mantra:
"I am That."

9 Become.

To become is very different from its cousin, the verb "to be". To be defines a state of present-moment-now-ness. To become denotes a change to the state of being-ness. Often times, we think of "becoming" as something that happens in the future but it is possible to stay grounded in the present moment and become more of who you are through awareness and deepening.

So much of being—and becoming—is about allowing. If you can sit quietly and allow yourself to open, you might allow your true-self to emerge. This emergence is the first step to becoming more of who you are. Once you show yourself, the next step is exploring and getting to know the real you. Who are you without your personality and pretense? What happens when you let down your façade? What happens when you give up and let yourself go? That is right, all of your false ego selves hold your life tightly wound. If you can unwind and allow your true self to emerge, I think you will find that you like the real you. "Finally," you will say. "Here I am!" Moreover, the subsequent conversations will be marvelous.

Exercise: Write a letter to the real you. You can write to your past or future versions and ask for guidance at any time. Next, write back, assuming the role of this past or future self. I think you'll be surprised at who you have become and the guidance your younger or older selves have for the present you.

Affirmation: I will drop the false pretenses of who I think I should be. I will allow my true being to step forward. My past and future selves will show me the way to who I am to become. I will focus on being in the present moment and allowing myself to bloom into full radiance. I will get to know the new me that emerges, as I continue along this healing journey. I will allow the great becoming.

Speak about BECOMING more of YOU.

What are qualities that are essential to me? If I did not have to battle fear and shame, what would I doing or feeling? Where would I be? What would my life look like?

As your life's co-creator, write your life into being.

(1.) _____

(2.) _____

(3.) _____

(4.) _____

(5.) _____

Listen. What messages emerge?

What other messages do I have about my healing journey of becoming? How do I practice being the person I wish to become?

?

?

?

?

?

?

?

?

?

Write about BECOMING.

The healing journey is all about becoming a better version of your most authentic self. Write a letter from your now self to your past- or future-self. What questions do you have? What guidance do you desire? Next, write back. What answers do you have to share? Write without thinking or analyzing. When your past or future self writes back, use your less dominant hand. It will help your ego-self step out of the way.

_____

_____

_____

_____

_____

_____

_____

_____

_____

_____

_____

_____

Draw your
BECOMING-NESS.

10 Believe.

To believe means to accept something as true. To believe in something means that you have an opinion that something is right or acceptable without having to justify it. It is very similar to having faith in something. I encourage you to believe yourself—trust yourself—and believe in yourself as much as you believe, trust, and believe in others. It is so easy to give your power away to others. Self-acceptance is critical in this work. Seeing yourself as an inherently good person will help you work through any feelings of shame that you might have built up inside. My husband said to me the other day, "Everything is not always your fault." What a relief!

This is about enough-ness. It is important to remind yourself that you are enough. Say, "I am enough." Repeat it. "I am enough." Then write it down on a little sticky note and put it on your bathroom mirror. In the morning or right before you go to bed, remind yourself that you are enough. You have said enough, you do enough, and you ARE enough. Being-ness just is. You don't have to do anything to be right here in the present moment. In fact, what must you STOP doing?!

Be YOU! Climb through the layers that your ego throws up around you as protection. Swim past the guard dogs and the barbed wire that keep other people at bay. Recognize your "fight, flight, freeze, or façade" response to being overwhelmed and disconnected and plug back into your Spirit or Higher Self. Tap into this part of yourself and you will increase your ability to trust and believe what you're up to and have great faith in what you stand for.

Affirmation: I am more than enough. I am willing to uncover the core of who I am so that I can tap into my inner-enough-ness. I will stand up for what I believe in.

Speak about your BELIEF system.

What makes up my belief system? Are there things that I believe that do not serve me?

Write down the things that you need to STOP believing.

(1.) _____

(2.) _____

(3.) _____

(4.) _____

(5.) _____

Listen. What messages emerge?

What other messages do I hold about believing in my own strength, power, courage, intelligence and aptitude? How can I feel satisfied with my efforts? How can I move forward without perfection? What other messages do I need to hear besides, "I am enough"?

?

?

?

?

?

?

?

Write about what it means to BELIEVE.

Write down 50 things you like about yourself. When I first did this exercise, it took me a long time to get started. Once I did start, the answers flowed. Allow your ego to get out of the way. Tell yourself what you appreciate. Once you're finished, read it aloud. Whenever you need a refresher about what you wish to believe about yourself, reread these messages here. Practice believing the ideas that are important to you or that you would like to believe.

_____

_____

_____

_____

_____

_____

_____

_____

_____

_____

Draw what you
BELIEVE.

11 Celebrate.

I was at work. I was working on an "above and beyond" project, meaning that it was outside of the scope of my job. In essence, I wasn't getting paid for doing it. The others that I was working with weren't getting paid for it either. As we were leaving the event, I turned to my colleague and said, "Thank you for your hard work." He stopped in his tracks. He paused and looked at me, stunned, "Laura, nobody has said thank you to me in nine years." What?! I will always remember this moment.

Celebration involves massive amounts of gratitude. It is the smallest of gestures to thank people for their efforts, ideas, contributions, and energy. I have a wonderful colleague who says, "Don't thank me yet..." when I thank her halfway through a project. I tell her, "I am going to thank you before, during, and afterwards!" Gratitude, I am certain, is indeed the very best attitude.

It is so easy to put your pedal to the metal and work, work, work. I often talk about being conscious about whether my words and actions are positive, like making deposits, or negative, like withdrawing money from an energetic bank account. If we are not careful, and do not pause to celebrate, we might pull out more energetic currency than we have stored up. No overdrawing! Take even five minutes each day to check in with your team to be thankful, have fun, smile, and share a cup of coffee. The difference will be noted and appreciated.

Affirmation: I will approach each day as a special day that requires reverence, appreciation, and celebration. I will wear my special clothing. I will greet people as if it is the last time I might see them. I am so thankful for all that I have, all the opportunities I have been given to be a better version of my best self. Today I will celebrate. Today I will appreciate. Today I will make sure I make as many energetic deposits to as many people as possible! Thank you!

Speak about deep play. Talk about CELEBRATION!

Write down five things that you will do this week to C E L E B R A T E !

(1.) _____

(2.) _____

(3.) _____

(4.) _____

(5.) _____

Listen. What messages emerge?

How do I create a sense of community around me? How do I build bonds with people? How do I remind myself of my own value and the value of others? How do I build unity in my community or at work?

?

?

?

?

?

?

?

?

Write it down. To CELEBRATE is to...

Write down how you like to celebrate. How do you like to receive appreciation? What are some successes that you have achieved? Are you someone who doesn't believe that there is time for fun and games? Why do you believe this? When did you stop knowing how to play? How do you play? How do you get extraordinary things done?

_____

_____

_____

_____

_____

_____

_____

_____

_____

_____

_____

_____

_____

Draw what it means to CELEBRATE.

12 Choose.

Not every year is great. A few years ago, I worked for a man who was very degrading to women, so I said so. Instead of holding him accountable for his behavior, I received retaliation for "telling on him." Feeling hopeless, I called a rape hotline. I can still remember the voice on the other end of the line. She reminded me that I am never stuck and that I always have choices. She helped me climb up out of a difficult situation and find my way to a better and brighter future. A Chinese acupuncturist once said to me, "Everything is workable." Even leaving an abusive work or home environment is workable. Even standing up to the bully who takes your lunch money is workable. Even getting out of bed today is workable.

Each day, I decide to come into work. I choose to be there. I get to be there and it is up to me whether or not I will do great work. It is up to me. What is significant is that you can ask yourself,

"What do I think I should do?" Tell yourself, "It's up to me." Remind yourself, "It's my decision." What if there were no way you could do it wrong? What if you couldn't mess things up? What if you couldn't fail? What then? Choices are required in order to experience success. Make sure to build them in for yourself, but also for your team and your family.

Try this exercise: Take an empty piece of paper. Write down what you require and desire. See what you write down. Then, you can work on making these things happen. Setting intentions follow the law of attraction. Once you announce them, the universe works to bring them to you. Make sure you are asking for what you really want!

Affirmation: I am never stuck. I always have choices. It is all workable. I am not what I do. My being-ness defines my worth and my value. My life is up to me.

Speak about CHOOSING.

Allow the questions to come. What does freedom of choice feel like? What would it feel like if I had the opportunity to exercise choice? What decisions can I make today? Pro-tip: I try not to make decisions when I am tired or hungry!

(1.) _____

(2.) _____

(3.) _____

(4.) _____

(5.) _____

Listen to the guidance of CHOOSING.

What are my next best right steps? What selections might I make today? What guidance can I give myself about my next best right step? What would happen if success were a guarantee? What would I do next?

?

?

?

?

?

?

?

Write it down.

Write down your life, as you would have it be. Throw fear to the wind. What would your life look like if you were not afraid? How would you design it? Really describe it. Make sure to flesh out the details. Go for it!

_____

_____

_____

_____

_____

_____

_____

_____

_____

_____

_____

_____

_____

_____

_____

_____

_____

Draw what it means
to CHOOSE.

13 Connect.

As much as we work very hard in life to connect with others, whether we key into our communication styles and practices at work, home, or in the community, be aware of your inner-connection with your inner being, or Higher Self, too.

How do you connect with your inner being? If you believe in God, you get in touch with your inner-you in very much the same way that you talk to God. Some believe that your Higher Self is God. As the co-creator in your life, you and God are in it together. Both your Higher Self and your Higher Power are creating the best for you. Expect abundance! Here are some pro tips:

(1.) Make sure you talk to your Higher Self and Higher Power in a way that makes you calm and comfortable. Be nice! Be reverent!

(2.) You may use a pen and paper to connect. This is a great exercise. I have written letters to my "Younger Self" and my "Older Self" asking my younger and older selves for guidance. I was indeed very surprised by the responses to my questions. You might also write to God. Try writing back from God without not controlling what comes. The answers will surprise you!

(3.) Watch your thinking! Fill your thoughts with Spirit or the Divine. You can read scripture from the Bible or another sacred text. My personal favorites are anything by Pema Chödrön or Thich Nhat Hanh. Their writing helps connect with the present moment and your inner-self.

Affirmation: I know my Higher Power and Higher Self are working in my best interest. I will expect abundance to come into my life. I will link up to the Divine.

Speak about CONNECTING.

Allow the questions to come.

If you could ask your inner-self anything, what would you ask?

(1.) _____

(2.) _____

(3.) _____

(4.) _____

(5.) _____

Listen. What messages emerge?

Listen for your inner voice. It might be silent or very faint at first, especially if you have experienced trauma. Sit quietly and listen. When your inner self feels trust, it will emerge. Put any messages that arise here.

?

?

?

?

?

?

?

?

Write about your inner-CONNECTION.

Dear Self,

_____

_____

_____

_____

_____

_____

_____

_____

_____

_____

_____

_____

_____

_____

_____

_____

_____

_____

_____

_____

_____

Love, Self

Draw CONNECTING with your Higher Self and/or your Higher Power.

14 Create.

To create means to bring something into existence. As the co-creator of your life, you are a master at this. Knowing this allows us to take responsibility for what happens to us. If you find yourself surrounded by negativity, then change your mindset and focus on gratitude. The most important parts about creating are starting and letting go of outcome.

Get started: You might have "perfection paralysis." Wanting it to be perfect for others, you feel overcome by anxiety, so you stall or stop. This clog prevents perfection from arriving. Guess what?! Perfection does not exist! You cannot screw this up. You cannot do this wrong. Creating is about allowing the creativity to flow through you... for your own satisfaction. Imagine yourself being a channel for the creative energy to come in. You are facilitating manifestation. Get yourself out of the way, remove others' perspectives, and allow your creation to show up. Just begin. Even if you shake or are fearful about the whole process. It is okay. It is like a muscle. It hurts at first, but with a little practice, you will get better at allowing.

Let go of outcome: So often, we plan backwards. "This is what I want," you might say. So, you plan and control the process based on the outcome you want. Creativity will often take a mind of its own. If you can begin without having the end in mind, I think you will be pleasantly surprised at what shows up. You may have heard the old adage, "It's the journey, not the destination." It helps you stay in the now and removes fear from the equation.

Affirmation: I am enough to create my life's masterpiece. I am worthy of creating brilliance. I have everything I require, desire, and deserve. I can channel positive energy to manifest beauty all around me, within me, and in my relationships.

Speak about CREATING your wonderful, special life.

Allow the questions to come. What will it take to create the life I want? What would I like to manifest in my life? Set your intentions here. Then, focus on them to help bring them about.

(1.) _____

(2.) _____

(3.) _____

(4.) _____

(5.) _____

Listen to the guidance of your own CREATIVITY.

What inspires you? What brings you joy? What excites you? What encourages you? Try to change your daily routine. Part of fostering creativity is managing stress. What does your body need? If you have too much on your mind, take a minute to write down what is consuming your mind-space. Make a list of creative ideas. If you do this daily for a while, you will come up with some great ideas. The more you do it, the more ideas will emerge.

?

?

?

?

Write it down.

Creative writing, in the form of poetry or fiction, allows you to use your imagination while writing. Feel free to look up creative writing prompts online to inspire you here. You could try your hand at poetry or a short story. Just keep writing.

_____

_____

_____

_____

_____

_____

_____

_____

_____

_____

_____

_____

_____

_____

_____

_____

_____

_____

Draw a self-portrait collage or create a vision board. What does self-CREATION look like?

15 Discover.

To discover means to find something unexpectedly. I like to imagine that in the course of finding something new there is a certain level of delight, which accompanies this encounter. What would it mean if you could discover something wonderful each day? Declare that you will spend time discovering newness around you. Then, watch what happens.

Without the pandemic, I recommend going somewhere you have never been before at least once a year. It does not have to be faraway or exotic, either. It might mean driving home from the supermarket a different way, or just getting lost. Head out without a destination and see where you end up. Then, try to find your way back home without using a map or your phone for help. This activity will activate your inner compass.

Realizing that the exterior terrain is just as vast as the interior is an enormous "aha-moment". As much as you might like to travel the world and see new places, you can do this on the spiritual, or metaphysical, plane too. In order to tap in, sit quietly and listen. When you use your inner-compass, it will show you the way. Prayer and gratitude are your currencies. Find your ,Stay the course.

Affirmation: I ask my inner-terrain to show itself to me. I ask my inner-compass to show me the way. I am grateful for all that has emerged in my life. I will look forward to trying something new, discovering a new place or a new way of doing something. I will become both the protagonist of my life but also an unemotional, objective observer, who can spot the route. Just like Ariadne did in the maze, I will leave a trail of yarn behind me, so I can always find my way out.

Speak about DISCOVERING your inner-terrain.

Allow the questions to come. What would you like to know about your inner-terrain? How do you travel? What would you take with you when you go? Is intergalactic travel possible? Do you bi-locate your presence in more than two places at once? How does this work? Does prayer help? Emotions are like weather in this case. What kind of weather does your inner-terrain experience? What about your thoughts? Do they calmly come and go, or do you hold onto them?

(1.) _____

(2.) _____

(3.) _____

(4.) _____

(5.) _____

Listen. What messages emerge?

Tap into your inner-guidance system, or your inner-compass. It may take a minute to get the hang of how you use it. Some call this intuition. Some call it asking for guidance from your Higher Self or Higher Power. Put any messages that arise here.

?

?

?

?

?

?

?

?

Write about using your inner compass to DISCOVER new lands.

Your inner compass is indeed a wonderful tool. Pay close attention. What is your "due North"? What is your "North Star", or the brightest star in your sky? What lights your way, no matter what?

_____
_____
_____
_____
_____
_____
_____
_____
_____
_____
_____
_____
_____
_____

Draw your latest DISCOVERY.

16 Dissolve.

When I think about dissolving, I often think about mixing salt or sugar in water. The salt or sugar is saturated and becomes a part of the water, or other substance, thereby creating a bitter or sweet taste to the wet solution. Dissolving also could mean that a larger crystal breaks into smaller crystals when it is exposed to a solvent. Each crystal still exists, just that more of the new crystals now surround them. How could "dissolving" work for you? What would you like to dissolve in your own life? How can you "swarm the project" to make a complicated task at work go more smoothly?

Here are several suggestions:

(1.)   Dissolving barriers.
(2.)   Dissolving limiting beliefs.
(3.)   Dissolving fear.
(4.)   Dissolving anger, sadness, and other difficult emotions.

You might work to surround the things that no longer serve you with more of the things that you want in your life. Dissolving requires patience and asking for what you really want. It also requires you to identify what your "solvent" is. What materials will open your energy centers (chakras) in your body? What will encourage healing?

Affirmation: I will allow more of what I want in my life to surround and transmute the things I do not want in my life. I will work to remove barriers and blockages that prevent my energy from flowing. I will work to push through fear and call my power back.

Speak about
DISSOLVING.

Allow the questions to come. What will it take to break things down in my life? What am I holding onto that no longer serves me? What areas can I increase, while others decrease? What can I minimize? What can I maximize?

(1.) _____

(2.) _____

(3.) _____

(4.) _____

(5.) _____

Listen. What messages emerge?

What other messages do I have about dissolving? Allow your Higher Self and/or Higher Power help identify some keys to dissolving. What are some key catalysts that will help spark movement and shift in your life?

?

?

?

?

?

?

?

?

Write about
DISSOLUTIONING.

Write about what you would like to transmute and change in your life. What would you like to reduce and shift? What are areas in our life that you would like to grow and maximize?

_____

_____

_____

_____

_____

_____

_____

_____

_____

_____

_____

_____

_____

_____

_____

_____

_____

Draw DISSOLVE.

17 Dream.

To dream is your mind creating stories and images while you sleep. Dreaming could be a way for your subconscious mind to help your conscious mind process what it is experiencing. All day, you absorb information. At night, this information is processed.

Daydreaming is a form of dreaming that occurs when you are still awake. It occurs when your mind wanders. You might replay something that happened in your head, think about your goals and aspirations, or imagine possible scenarios for your life.

Dream interpretation is a fun and helpful practice of understanding the meanings of your dreams. These meanings offer confirmation to the experiences in your waking life. If you can remember your dreams, try writing them down when you first wake up. It is helpful to keep a journal and pen beside your bed for just such a purpose. Then, extract the symbols or objects that appear during your dream. You can look up the symbols in a dream dictionary. You will learn more about the undercurrents of your mind, what you are processing, and more about how you feel.

Dreams improve your creativity and help with problem solving. They help access a kind of intelligence that is not always available in your wakeful experience. They help tap into the untapped potential of your psyche and give you resilience. They restore your vibrancy.

Affirmation: I will be sure to spend time sleeping so that I might have access to my dreams. Upon waking up, I will tap into their intelligence. I will learn more about the inner workings of my psyche. I will watch what comes up to know more about what my shadow side is processing. I will allow myself to rest so that I might have greater access to my creativity, emotions, and imagination.

Speak about your DREAMS.

Allow yourself to put your dreams and aspirations on paper. Once you verbalize them, ASK them to arrive, FOCUS on them, and ALLOW them to enter your experience. Put them here for safekeeping. What do your dreams tell you? Put their messages or questions here for safe-keeping.

(1.) _____

(2.) _____

(3.) _____

(4.) _____

(5.) _____

Listen. What messages emerge?

What do you dreams tell you? Have people visited you in your dreams? List them here. What messages do your dreams give you?

Are loved ones who have passed on come to see you in your sleep? What have they come to say to you?

?

?

?

?

?

?

?

Write about DREAMING.

Use this space to begin journaling about your dreams. When you wake up and remember your dream, write down what you observe. Circle the objects and symbols that you have just recorded. Then, look them up in a dream dictionary. You might then spend some time journaling about what you have just discovered. Connect your sleeping intelligence with your wakeful knowledge. You may find some incredibly helpful connections about relationships or next steps for your life.

_____
_____
_____
_____
_____
_____
_____
_____
_____
_____

Draw your greatest
DREAM.

18 Dwell.

To dwell means to reside, to live. Are you living presently or are you checked out? The idea of "the pause" is included in this action word. May you practice a slight pause every now and then in the flow and motion of your life. A pause helps you collect yourself, pulling together your ideas, attitudes, feelings, and beliefs. A pause allows time to process, and it holds your attention for a longer period. Take a breath. Digest what is on your plate before you move on.

Dwell can also mean, "To dwell on" something. What are you dwelling on? What are you choosing to focus on? Where are you placing your attention?

Attention → Feelings → Thoughts → Actions

Your life is your dwelling and your home. Have you made your life into a home, or is it still just a building? Take a look around. What needs fixing? What can you take to the thrift store or throw away? What is not needed?

At the same time, what makes your life-dwelling beautiful? How are you to decorate your life? With joy and abundance, forgiveness and courage? Or, are you focused on their counterparts? The best part is that you get to choose what you bring into your life and what you do not require. You can do this every day.

Affirmation: I am allowed to let my foot off the gas every now and then. I am allowed to get up from my desk every now and then and go for a walk. I am allowed to clean up the clutter in my life. I am safe to create a beautiful experience. I have the time to create a home in my life. I dwell in and on gratitude and positivity. My life is a joyous experience. If it isn't currently, I know that I am moving in that direction with purpose. I am free to take a breath. Or two.

Speak about
DWELLING-NESS.

Allow the questions to come. What will it take to make my life beautiful? How might I simplify my experience? Here are five (or more) questions that I ask about radical acceptance.

(1.) _____

(2.) _____

(3.) _____

(4.) _____

(5.) _____

Listen. What messages emerge?

What other messages do I receive about practicing the pause or where I am placing my focus? What are my next best right steps?

Create a list of more verbs to help you dwell beautifully in your life.

?

?

?

?

?

?

?

Write about what it means to DWELL.

Write down how you see your life, as if it were your dwelling. What does your life (place) look like? This isn't literal so much as it is figurative. What thoughts, behaviors, or emotions are you holding onto that no longer serve you? How can you dwell more presently?

_____

_____

_____

_____

_____

_____

_____

_____

_____

_____

_____

_____

_____

_____

_____

Draw your life's
DWELLING.

19 Elevate.

"To elevate" is like the verb "to rise." Two ideas here: go above the cloud cover and lift your vibrational frequency to increase your peace of mind. Here are two scenarios to help you imagine increasing your own elevation:

(1.) Imagine that you are in an airplane. The weather is cloudy and all you can see are gray skies. When you take off, the pilot flies the plain to a higher elevation. In the process, the plane moves through the clouds, only to emerge above them. When you elevate, you move through your own clouds, whether they are emotional or attitudinal. On a teabag tab at the end of the string was this message: "You are the sky. The rest is just weather." This could not be truer.

(2.) How do you raise your vibration? Imagine that you are a string on a guitar and violin. When a string is plucked, it moves back and forth very quickly creating a buzzed humming sound. It will vibrate until it becomes very still. What in your life will be the pluck for you? Is it yoga, meditation, or going for a long walk? Is it finding a quiet, recharging moment in the morning before everyone else wakes up? Is it writing in your gratitude journal about all of your many blessings?

In order to elevate your energy, become aware of your thoughts and feelings. Find something to appreciate in your immediate surroundings. Drink water to flush your system. Meditate to clear your mind. Initiate an act of kindness for someone else. Exercise. All of these things will help raise your frequency. In doing so, you will lift your spirits.

Affirmation: Repeat after me, "I am the sky. The rest is just weather."

Speak about ELEVATING my energy.

Allow the questions to come. What will it take to lift my spirits? How might I elevate my frequency? Here are five (or more) questions that I ask about radical acceptance.

(1.) _____

(2.) _____

(3.) _____

(4.) _____

(5.) _____

Listen. What messages emerge?

What messages do I have about increasing my elevation? Let the messages emerge about elevating my life to the next level. What is needed?

?

?

?

?

?

?

?

?

?

Write about what it means to ELEVATE.

Write about how you can elevate your own mindset and raise your own frequency. What will it take to lift your spirits? What will it take to put you in a positive frame of mind? How can you calm your emotions? What small act of care can you implement for your own piece of mind?

_____

_____

_____

_____

_____

_____

_____

_____

_____

_____

_____

_____

_____

_____

_____

Draw your
ELEVATION.

20 Endure.

Sometimes our healing process takes longer than we think it should. It might feel harder than expected. Endurance is a very critical component in the healing process. To endure means to suffer patiently through something. I wonder if "suffering patiently," means that we are able to stay present with our grief, to move through our anger with grace and indeed so much patience. I wonder if it means that we know that the mountain we are climbing will not last forever. Eventually, we will reach our apex and be able to move onto a different lesson and climb a different hill. Emotions are like weather. It is as if we are waiting for the current thunderstorm to blow over before continuing on our journey.

There is another part to the definition. "To suffer patiently without yielding." The opposite of yield means to flow, or to allow. Allowing yourself to take the path of least resistance, to go with the flow, is also part of enduring. Might we get ourselves out of our own way, moving our ego (yield) out of the way of our Spirit (flow).

Endurance requires strength as well. Strength comes from the divine. Might you tap into your eternal pool of strength needed to move through any given situation, whether it is a difficult day that you are having, or is as daunting as grieving a death in your family. Knowing that you have access to all the power needed is indeed a relief.

Affirmation: I allow my ego to get out of my Spirit's way, to let things flow along with the path of least resistance. I remind myself that this too shall pass. That what I am going through is temporary. I have access to all the strength I need to endure today, tomorrow, and the day after that. I am doing well in my journey.

Speak about ENDURANCE.

What has felt difficult that I have had to spend many moons working through? What areas of my life require a great deal of strength? Where do I feel I need to focus my energy?

(1.) _____

(2.) _____

(3.) _____

(4.) _____

(5.) _____

Listen. What messages emerge?

What other messages do I hear about my own endurance? What guidance do I have for myself about how to stay present with any difficulty I might be experiencing?

?

?

?

?

?

?

?

?

?

Write about ENDURANCE.

Spend some time writing about your strength. How have you overcome adversity in your life? What are some triumphs that bring you the most pride? Describe some works in progress. Where is your healing energy required? What requires your focus?

_____

_____

_____

_____

_____

_____

_____

_____

_____

_____

_____

_____

_____

_____

_____

_____

Draw it. How does
ENDURE show up?

21 Evolve.

To evolve means to develop gradually over an extended period of time. Spiritually, it might mean that you move into a more advanced state of bliss or feel more connected with God, or your Higher Power. When something evolves, it changes. The Latin word, evolvere, means "to unroll."

Unroll your mat. Evolve your spiritual connection. Set aside some time to "unroll" your yoga mat and sit quietly for a few minutes before you do some yoga poses. This practice will help connect your mind, spirit, and body.

Unroll, or evolve in, the Word. You might also envision the Bible, or another sacred text, written on scrolls. In order to connect with divine guidance, "unroll" the scripture. Access the divine blessings and healings that are always available to you.

Unroll your inbox. Evolve your clutter. Perhaps you have heard of the app called "Unroll.Me." The app goes through your inbox and helps you unsubscribe from emails that are no longer of interest to you. Reduce your electronic clutter. It will help you focus your time and effort on the things you want.

As you work to evolve, think holistically, merging your spirituality and biology. Make sure to meet your basic needs first. Ask for help as needed here. Many organizations are in place to help you close your basic loops. Then, focus on your higher realities. They will open up to you as you work to align your energetic chakra system, or connect with God. Working to balance your energy system and raise your vibrational frequency will help connect your biological and spiritual experiences.

Affirmation: I will make time to connect my mind, body, and spirit. I will unroll in as many ways that are revealed to me.

Speak about EVOLVING, or unrolling.

List several activities that will connect your physical experience with your spiritual life. For example, you might write in your gratitude journal every morning, practice yoga for 10 minutes before going to bed, or go for a walk at lunch. Evolution takes action.

(1.) _____

(2.) _____

(3.) _____

(4.) _____

(5.) _____

Listen to my spiritual EVOLUTION.

What are my next best right steps? As I change, what inner guidance do I receive?

Create a list of more verbs to help you unroll and evolve into the next best version of your best self.

?

?

?

?

?

?

?

?

Write it down.

Write down how you have gradually changed. You might want to discuss which ways you have changed since experiencing the pandemic. What changes have accelerated? What have you had to adjust to move more quickly? What has stayed the same?

_____

_____

_____

_____

_____

_____

_____

_____

_____

_____

_____

_____

_____

_____

_____

_____

_____

Draw it.

22 Experience.

When was the last time that you got up early and observed the sunrise from its slumber? When was the last time that you simply sat and read a book or went on a long walk in nature?

Life is all about your experiences. Each experience holds one or many lessons for you. If you are so busy, you are not present mentally, spiritually, emotionally, or physically. You might miss the opportunity altogether.

Experiencing is about living moment-to-moment and having awareness of the internal and external events that make up your life. Life is about noticing what is around you. Some will look at the big-ness, while others will focus on the small details. Both are revealing, as long as you are paying attention.

Another question that may arise: "Do you have experience with abc or xyz?" It is important to remember that what you have done in the past will not necessarily prepare you for the future. Imagine that you are going to school for jobs that do not exist yet. The technology hasn't been invented. The ideas haven't emerged just yet. Being willing to learn as if you are a beginner is a refreshing mindset.

Experiences make up your character or the fabric of your life. Today, see what comes up. Ask, what precious moment might I hold dear? What will I notice today?

Affirmation: I will allow myself to live moment-to-moment today. I will notice all that is around me, first, with what I can see, what I can hear, and what I can smell. I will hold my favorite blanket in my hand and feel its texture. I will experience the warmth of the sun, or the cold of the winter wind. Today is for me.

Speak about EXPERIENCING.

Allow the questions to come. What do I notice around me? How do I feel? Here are five (or more) questions that I ask about the small moments of my life.

(1.) _____

(2.) _____

(3.) _____

(4.) _____

(5.) _____

Listen. What messages emerge?

What other messages do I notice about my experience? What are my next best right steps?

Create a list of special experiences that you would like to have.

?

?

?

?

?

?

?

?

Write about
EXPERIENCING.

Write down your most memorable experience to date. Next, think about now. What did you experience today? What are you experiencing right in this moment? What did you learn from each experience? What do you need to do to quiet your life? How will you allow your inner-guide to emerge? What will lead you to new experiences?

_____

_____

_____

_____

_____

_____

_____

_____

_____

_____

_____

_____

_____

Draw EXPERIENCE. How does moment-to-moment look like?

23 Flow.

To flow means to move in a steady, continuous stream. It can also means to be "in the zone" or "in the groove." A flow state is an actual psychological term to describe a state of energized focus, full involvement, and enjoyment all at the same time. Read anything by Mihály Csikszentmihályi, a Hungarian-American psychologist, who in 1975 named this concept of Flow—or a highly focused mental state that is helpful for productivity.

You will experience more happiness when you are in a state of Flow. Here are some essential components of "going with the flow." In your greatest flow state, you will be:

(1.)   Internally motivated.
(2.)   In full-concentration-mode.
(3.)   Completely involved.
(4.)   Merging awareness plus actions.
(5.)   Balancing your skill level and the challenge at hand.

How do you get into your FLOW? Choose your work that you love. Make sure your work is challenging but not too hard. Discover your best working time. Are you most fresh first thing in the morning? Are you brilliant late at night? Enjoy yourself. Spend as long as possible working on the task, so you can find your focus.

Affirmation: I accept peaceful, productive abundance into my life. I allow love to flow freely. I love my work. It is uplifting and effortless. I find time to play.

Speak about FLOW.

What are some things that I experience when I am in my flow state? When does it move often occur? What am I working on when it happens?

Go into observation mode so you can try to replicate it as often as possible. Record your notes here.

(1.) _____

(2.) _____

(3.) _____

(4.) _____

(5.) _____

Listen to the guidance of your FLOW.

Feel the flow of energy. I accept things in my life to flow. I am in flow. I am THE FLOW. I let go of control and allow. What guidance do you have for yourself about getting into your state of flow?

?

?

?

?

?

?

?

Write down your distractions so you can FLOW.

In order to flow, you will need to eliminate all outside distractions. Reclaim your time—close your inbox, clear your schedule. Use this space to "brain-dump" and put all of your distractions and thoughts that are occupying your headspace.

_____

_____

_____

_____

_____

_____

_____

_____

_____

_____

_____

_____

_____

_____

_____

_____

Draw your flow state. How does it look?

24 Follow.

One of the most important parts of leading is the ability to follow. Even Aristotle knew this. He said, "(S)he who cannot be a good follower, cannot be a good leader." To follow means to move or travel behind. You will want your team to proceed ahead of you. Leadership is not about you. It is about getting out of your own way so that success can happen.

To be a good follower, you must have trust in the abilities of your (inner) leader. Therefore, you must ultimately believe in yourself and your own abilities. Have confidence that you know what you are doing. Always be willing to ask for help if you do not. Boosting trust, over-communication, and compassion are keys that are critically important now more than ever. Self-love and self-care are necessary too.

Just like leadership, followership can influence the success and ultimate effectiveness of an organization. To be a good follower means that you lead from where you are. I talk a lot about "bottom-up leadership" or "sideways leadership", meaning "managing up" or "peer-to-peer influencing" respectively. You can always influence and create greatness from wherever you are. Your energy matters.

Following may include what you follow as well as whom you follow. What are your personal mission and vision statements? Where does your inner-compass tell you to go? What is your life's purpose? What are your personal passions? Many of the answers to these questions will determine what, how, and whom you follow.

Affirmation: I will focus on leading from where I am. I will always put my team first. I believe in my abilities and myself. I will have confidence to know what I need to know and ask for help when I do not. I will follow my own inner-guidance, remember my personal passion and purpose, and remember that I am loved and so very essential.

Speak about willingness to FOLLOW.

Being willing to follow takes as much finesse as leadership. What will it take to be a good follower? Here are five (or more) areas that I would like to work on. For example, I would like to check my ego at the door. What else?

(1.) _____

(2.) _____

(3.) _____

(4.) _____

(5.) _____

Listen. What messages emerge?

What are my intentions as a follower? What concepts do you believe that you will follow both courageously and confidently?

?

?

?

?

?

?

?

?

?

Write about FOLLOWER-SHIP.

Like leadership, follower-ship is just as essential. Leadership is nothing more than being a great follower of something you believe in that is bigger than yourself. Write about whom, what, and how you follow.

WHO do I follow?

_____

_____

_____

WHAT do I follow?

_____

_____

_____

HOW do I follow?

_____

_____

_____

Draw what it means to FOLLOW.

25 Forgive.

Forgiveness is one of the most difficult actions to take. At the same time, it is the most rewarding and helpful. When you hold a grudge, you carry around negativity. Whether it feels warranted by events that occurred or by words that were spoken, in reality these details do not matter. What matters is that you let go of these feelings you're gripping. Forgiveness is not about them. It is about self-love.

You may have allowed these feelings and emotions to seep into your body. Perhaps they have surfaced as illness or injury. Be gentle with yourself and allow them stay with you until you are ready to let them go. It is okay that you are feeling the way you are feeling. However, this is an invitation to loosen your grip. Hold the person's face in front of you and send them love.

Forgiveness saves you, not them. Let go of your anger so you can be free. How do you forgive? Where do you start? Forgiveness begins with you. What if this whole kerfluffle had nothing to do with them? What if it had everything to do with the way you experience the other person? Forgive your thinking about the other person.

Review what happened. What role did you play? What responsibility can you take for what happened? Project positivity in order to receive it. The imagery of a duck's features is helpful here. They are coated with a layer of oil. When submerged in water, the feathers are protected. Allow yourself to be protected by grace or your sense of divinity in order to be protected from negativity.

Affirmation: Today I will forgive myself for being human. Today I will forgive myself for making mistakes, for thinking ill-willed thoughts, or for creating transgressions. Today I will take responsibility for my own words and actions.

Speak about radical FORGIVENESS.

Allow the questions to come. What needs to be forgiven today? What do I need to let go? Here are five (or more) questions that I ask about forgiveness.

(1.) _____

(2.) _____

(3.) _____

(4.) _____

(5.) _____

Listen. What messages emerge?

What will I forgive today? What are my next best right steps?

Create a list of places where you are giving away my power.

?

?

?

?

?

?

?

?

Write it down. To FORGIVE is to...

Write down what you have yet to forgive and list the names of those you would like to forgive. Get it out, and write it down. Let go. Keep these emotions front and center. Try to feel your feelings, and let them run their course. Write them down. Now, let them go. (This may take some time, and you may want to revisit this writing prompt on more than one occasion.)

_____

_____

_____

_____

_____

_____

_____

_____

_____

_____

_____

_____

_____

Draw FORGIVING.
What does it look
like? More
importantly, how do
you feel?

26 Generate.

To generate means to cause something to arise or come about. So, how do you bring something about? And, what do you bring about? You are responsible for what you bring about, for your energy, and for your own attitude. Your response to whatever comes up is yours. The most wonderful part is that you get to decide what kind of response it will be.

You can also generate ideas. The good old brainstorming session helps keep your mind and your ideas fresh. Pick a topic and set a timer. Then, "Ready, set, go!" Just start writing. Come up with as many new ideas as you can within the time limit. You might try to do this daily. Create a safe space for yourself to generate ideas. The more you do it, the better you will become at generating ideas on the fly.

You cannot force what you want to come about. It works much better if you ask, focus on what you desire, and then allow it to show up. If you are able to let go, rather than holding on tightly to control, I think you will notice better results.

Bringing about energy or ideas takes tenacity and follow-through. Make decisions and stick with them. It is also okay to abandon ideas, belief systems, or behaviors that no longer serve you. It is also okay to stick with something you radically believe. When you finish something, you can build on it. You will also feel a sense of accomplishment. Cheer yourself on! You can do it! You can bring about positivity.

Affirmation: I am responsible for the energy I bring. I am responsible for the attitude I have in each of my situations. I have the power to bring about new ideas and manifest them. I can achieve anything I desire. I am worthy of generating new and positive ideas.

Speak about GENERATING greatness.

Allow the questions to come. What is needed today? What needs to come about? How can I help manifest them?

(1.) _____

(2.) _____

(3.) _____

(4.) _____

(5.) _____

Listen. What messages emerge?

Removing all fear, thoughts of nay-saying, and shoulds, have-tos, and musts, what energy remains? How does my joy show up today? What positivity can I muster? What great things might I intend for today?

?

?

?

?

?

?

?

?

Write it down. What would you like to generate?

Think of a topic. Set a timer for a few minutes. Then, "Ready, set, go!" Write down as many ideas as you can. Then, look at what you have generated. I think you will be surprised at all the great ideas that have sprung forth!

_____

_____

_____

_____

_____

_____

_____

_____

_____

_____

_____

_____

_____

_____

Draw
GENERATING.
What does it look like
to create ideas,
energy, and
attitudes?

27 Grow.

Grow where you are planted. I remember this still. I was living in Los Angeles, California at the time. I was going through a drive-thru for dinner one night when I saw the most beautiful flower blooming in all its glory on the side of the drive-thru lane. The message, "Grow where you are planted," came so strongly, as if the flower were saying it to me itself. I have remembered this message still as I find myself buried in my own life. A seed, I am getting ready to grow into a beautiful flower.

Growth takes courage. Inside the seed contains the beautiful flower, or the tall tree. Before we embark on the journey of personal growth, the idea of our greatest version of ourselves is already conceived. We just need to carry ourselves to term. Along my walks, I often see plants growing in between the cracks of the sidewalk. It must have taken great courage to push through a hard surface (read: fear) to feel the open air (read: "Everything we want is on the opposite side of fear." —Will Smith). Bloom. Allow your beauty to come shining through, no matter what else is occurring.

Just like a caterpillar, sometimes we must come completely undone before we can experience the great transformation – a metamorphosis – morphing into completely new versions of ourselves. When the time is right, we will crawl out of our cocoons and emerge triumphantly.

Affirmation: There is a reason why there are growing pains, for if we were comfortable, we would not be growing. I am willing to grow right where I am. I have the courage to break through the blanket of fear. I am open and available to growing up, to growing old, to growing into the best version of my best self.

Speak about GROWING.

Allow the questions to come. What needs to be cultivated in your life? What needs to be weeded out? Here five (or more) questions that I ask about growth.

(1.) _____

(2.) _____

(3.) _____

(4.) _____

(5.) _____

Listen. What messages emerge?

Imagine yourself crawling into a dark, comfortable cocoon. Allow all of what you know to come apart. Allow yourself to be put back together again. As you emerge, you will realize that you are completely new. What message emerge about your new self?

?

?

?

?

?

?

?

Write it down. To GROW is to...

How do I experience growth in my own life?

_____

_____

_____

_____

_____

_____

_____

_____

_____

_____

_____

_____

_____

_____

_____

_____

_____

_____

_____

_____

_____

_____

Draw yourself
GROWING.

28 Guide.

We have been well trained to seek external third party sources for validation—and guidance. As the hero or heroine of our adventure, there is always a moment where we are the muse to ourselves, "And (s)he did not know what to do." We then must seek out a credible, trusted advisor to show us our next best right step. What if we could be that trusted advisor for ourselves? If the journey of leadership is to be spiritual in nature and an inside job, there is nobody more qualified. I hope you accept the job offer!

The first thing that must occur is ASK. The next part of the equation is to ALLOW. We often ASK, but then put up construction sites over every off ramp. Make it easy on yourself and get out of your own way. Allow the manifestation to occur. Be patient as the next step reveals itself. Allowance and patience are key components to receiving guidance. Focus on what you want. So often, you might ask for what you want, but then you will focus on what you do not want. What do you think comes into your experience? YES! More of what you do not want!

There are also spirit guides, which are very similar to angels. Sometimes, if you have lost a baby (s)he will become your spirit guide. Other loved ones might also do the same thing. I was reading a book, which suggested calling a meeting with your spirit guides and asking for guidance. Of course, I tried this while driving down the highway! Sure enough, I told my guides, "Get in here!", and they all came!

Affirmation: I am my own best guide for how I am to live my life. I will ask, allow, and receive with gratitude. I will feel comfortable asking my spirit guides for guidance. I will remember that I am the co-creator of my life.

Speak about being your own GUIDE.

Allow the questions to come. As the inner-guide of your life, what guidance do you have to share with yourself about the direction of your life? You might isolate a specific occurrence and show guidance specific to that moment.

(1.) _____

(2.) _____

(3.) _____

(4.) _____

(5.) _____

Listen. What messages emerge?

Be still and take a few deep breaths. Allow your inner guide to speak to you. Put your own wisdom just here. You will be able to refer to it later, especially whenever you feel doubt or guilt.

?

?

?

?

?

?

?

?

Write about GUIDANCE.

Bringing divine energy into the physical plane through action is the role that I play in co-creating my life. How might I help manifest my life, as I would have it? Be specific in the details. This is part of the ASKING process. Once you ask, allow, focus, and say thank you.

_____

_____

_____

_____

_____

_____

_____

_____

_____

_____

_____

_____

_____

_____

Draw GUIDANCE.
What do your spirit
guides look like?

29 Heal.

To heal means to either become whole again or alleviate an ailment. Both are important ideas. To experience a healing is to experience total peace and wellness within our bodies, minds, and spirits. Many of us are walking around with a very real, very scary illness or chronic disease. Many of us have experienced trauma in our lives, whether emotional, mental, spiritual, or physical. And, most recently, we or our loved ones might have contracted COVID-19. Perhaps our loved ones have passed away recently. Perhaps the going has gotten really tough.

Co-healing is a wonderful concept to think about and to put into practice. If you can begin to take responsibility for your thoughts, feelings, and actions, then you will not need to put them into your body as unaddressed messages or send them out as projections onto other people. Our bodies send us messages. They are the most intelligent, wonderful vessels. These messages are cues for us to phone in divine intervention to support our healing processes. Other people are also messages for us to tune in to the power within and _HEAL_.

Healing takes a great deal of energy. You have to access the infinite healing power within in order to heal. Your Higher Power will also help you heal. This process starts with you eliminating distractions. Turn off your phone, turn off your technology, and really connect with yourself. Plug into your own healing power. What are the messages available to you?

Affirmation: I am already whole and well. I am safe to show my wounds. Once I can show my wounds, I can heal them. My Higher Power sees me in my whole, well-being-ness. I am safe to be my full self. I am happy, whole, and well. I am capable of healing my wounds and my illnesses with the help of my divine Higher Power.

Speak about HEALING.

Allowing the questions to come, what will it take to experience wholeness? Here are five (or more) questions that I ask about the healing power in my life.

(1.) _____

(2.) _____

(3.) _____

(4.) _____

(5.) _____

Listen. What messages emerge?

What other messages do I have about healing and wholeness? What are my next best right steps? Create a list of more verbs to help you move back to center.

?

?

?

?

?

?

?

?

?

Write about HEALING oneself.

The first step in healing is identifying the problem. Take a listen and look inside. What is going on in there? What doesn't feel right? What feels scary? What needs to be healed? Be honest with yourself. Whatever arises, treat it with love and great care. Gentleness might just be the order of the day.

_____

_____

_____

_____

_____

_____

_____

_____

_____

_____

_____

_____

_____

_____

Draw what it means to HEAL. What does it look like? Allow the healing to occur.

30 Influence.

To influence is to have an effect on someone's character, development, or behavior. It is also possible to influence a situation, strategy, or idea. Some might believe that to influence something is equivalent to manipulating or maneuvering. As Shakespeare wrote in Hamlet's Act 2, Scene 2, "why, then, 'tis none to you, for there is nothing either good or bad, but thinking makes it so." Intention and purpose are critical. What are you influencing? And why? Are you doing it for a positive, beneficial reason, or is it ego-driven? This is what makes the difference.

In a business sense, influence or persuasion often occurs with and through people in a friendly, supportive way. The goal is to align points of view and objectives. It takes a great deal of optimism and motivation included in using influence to move business forward. A great catalyst like influence quickly changes behavior and makes decisions possible on the fly. You do not need to be the lead leader to influence. The art of persuasion is all about cutting through the noise in order to simplify the message only to include essentials. It also includes communicating sincere concern and care for the topic at hand.

The idea of "spiritual influence" is indeed very powerful. It will provide you an incredible support system as you work with others in your organization. Influence is about creating IMPACT. Be great at what you do, but do it with authenticity. You will inspire trust and confidence as a result...thereby changing behavior and inspiring cohesion, cooperation, and consideration. Think about the leaders you admire. What would they do in this situation? How would they respond?

Affirmation: I will use my skill and competencies to instill confidence. I will act from a place of great sincerity to inspire trust. I will work to create great, life-changing IMPACT!

Speak INFLUENCE into being.

Write down several characteristics one would need to create consideration. What beliefs are necessary for people to come along with an idea?

How might you bring you expertise and talents to the table to help?

(1.) _____

(2.) _____

(3.) _____

(4.) _____

(5.) _____

Listen. What messages emerge?

Where is your energy required? Where might you be focusing your energy? Where is your positivity and positioning needed?

Allow yourself to write openly and see what emerges here.

?

?

?

?

?

?

?

?

Write about creating INFLUENCE.

What are some things that you care about? Why are they important to you? What are some things that need your skillset and competencies? What are some things that need your confidence and creativity? How will you create IMPACT? How will you influence others also to create impact?

_____

_____

_____

_____

_____

_____

_____

_____

_____

_____

_____

_____

_____

_____

Draw the impact of
INFLUENCE.

31 Lead.

I have always believed that leadership happens from wherever you are. Whether you are leading top-down, bottom-up, or sideways, you have incredible influence over what happens to you and others on any given day. You do not have to be a CEO to lead! I started my work with leadership almost 15 years ago. I think it took off in earnest when I read The Leadership Challenge by James Kouzes and Barry Posner (2007). Their book reveals five leadership practices of exemplary leadership:

(1.) Model the Way
(2.) Inspire a Shared Vision
(3.) Challenge the Process
(4.) Enable Others to Act
(5.) Encourage the Heart

These five practices have shaped the way I lead, and I still work on them today. Kouzes and Posner reminded me that "leadership is a relationship."

Independently, in my quest for all things spiritual, I found that leadership is also an inside job. If I could get clear on my personal vision and mission statement, then I could up my integrity game, and move my life forward in the way that I intended. Leadership is a relationship. Indeed it is. I think leadership is, at its very core, a relationship with the Self. They say, "Leadership development is self-development."

Affirmation: I am the CEO of my life. I will work on doing what I say I will do. I will work on modeling my follow-through. I will work on honoring what is right in front of me. I will work on opening up to the creativity and innovation in my life. I will let my ideas flow freely. I will treat my work and life as great adventures. As the co-creator of my life, I will inspire. I will celebrate. I will step outside of my comfort zone. I will make sure I confirm my values. I will trust.

Speak LEADERSHIP into being.

Write down several leaders whom you admire. Why did they make the list? What about them makes them special? Why are they exemplary?

(1.) _____

(2.) _____

(3.) _____

(4.) _____

(5.) _____

Listen. What messages emerge?

What does love have to do with leadership? Leadership is about staying present with a challenge. Leadership is about staying present with yourself and others in difficult situations. What does hope have to do with leadership?

?

?

?

?

?

?

?

?

Write about LEADING.

Write your leadership practice here. What are some of your personal tenents when it comes to leadership? As you think about your future, how might you step up and out to lead? What tools will you need? What motivation will you need to take the helm? Why not you? Why not now?

_____

_____

_____

_____

_____

_____

_____

_____

_____

_____

_____

_____

_____

_____

_____

Draw LEADERSHIP.

32 Learn.

I am a lifelong learner, one who is always willing to learn something new. Learning takes willingness to stumble through something for a while until you get the hang of it. That is where the magic can be found. Is there something that you used to do as a child that you would like to continue? When I was seven, I started taking karate. I cannot remember why I stopped. When my daughter started taking Tae Kwan Do, I sat in the waiting room one time watching her. It looked like too much fun to miss out. I remember the first time I put my gear on and sparred with another parent who was also in the family class. "Wow! This is wonderful fun!" My daughter and I proceeded to earn our first-degree black belts over the course of three years. The discipline, obedience, and confidence that emerged because of the consistent practice were amazing. Especially right now, as the world reinvents itself, how will you reinvent yourself? What would you really like to be doing? What would you like to learn how to do? Learn French? Ride a motorcycle? Go for it!

The other part about learning involves deeper, more essential lessons. I often think that the spiritual or energetic learnings I came here to learn in this lifetime keep showing up until I really learn them. Have you ever left a company because of someone that you could not stand, only to find the same kind of person at your new place of employment? Perhaps you struggle with establishing boundaries in each relationship you enter. Why is that? Whatever the case, you will be confronted with the work until you face and deal with it. The minute you say, "Stop!" it will cease to continue! Pay attention to your patterns of struggle.

Affirmation: I am open to learning new things. I will seek out the opportunities that interest me and that give me the opportunity to have fun. I will spend time observing the patterns of my life to see what I must discover and affirm.

Speak about LEARNING something new.

What are some things that you would like to learn? If you have ever said, "I wish I knew how to..." or "I always wish I had learned how to...", then these are great things to write down here. How would you like your life to look? What are skills required to get you there?

(1.) _____

(2.) _____

(3.) _____

(4.) _____

(5.) _____

Listen. What spiritual lessons emerge?

Go outside and look up at the stars. This practice will remind you that there is something larger than you are. As you embark, or continue, along your spiritual journey of learning, what questions emerge? In communicating with the spiritual plane, what messages are revealed for you? Allow yourself to write whatever is uncovered.

?

?

?

?

?

?

?

Write about
LEARNING.

Write about some patterns that you notice in your life. Perhaps people deem it appropriate to interrupt you when you are speaking. Maybe you are great at interviewing for positions but you do not stay very long. Why is that? Spend some time thinking deeply about how the "Wheel of Samsara," or the cycling of suffering, show up for you. How might you breathe more consciousness into each scenario?

_____

_____

_____

_____

_____

_____

_____

_____

_____

_____

_____

_____

Draw LEARNING.

33 Listen.

My dear friend always says, "If your mouth is moving, then it is a story about you." After he said this, I have never really talked in quite the same way. This message has allowed me to listen to my own stories about me, as well as the stories that I tell about others. Even the stories about others are really still all about me. Listening is an important part of leadership. To listen means to give your attention to a sound or idea. Being a good listener takes practice. There is an activity called "Mirror Listening." You are not allowed to ask questions when you "mirror". You can only repeat back what you think you have heard. The speaker will confirm or clarify until they feel as though you have captured what they were saying. Try using a phrase like, "So what I am hearing you say is…" Questions control narrative to shape the way you wish to hear something. Realizing that sometimes you might be listening only so you can respond is also eye-opening. This is another form of control. It is time to let go and spend time really listening.

Some pro-tips for good listening:

(1.) Make sure to make eye contact.
(2.) Relax and stay in the now-ness of what you are hearing.
(3.) Stay open. You might be hearing something that you disagree with, and that is okay! You can still be present.
(4.) Do not interrupt or problem-solve. Not everything requires a solution. Sometimes, you just need to stop and listen.

Affirmation: When I listen, I will really listen, staying in the present moment.

Speak about LISTENING.

What are some ways that you might improve your listening skills? Practice keeping your focus. When your favorite song comes on during someone's story, do not say, "Oh, I love this song." Stay present. Perhaps you could try sharing your ideas after they share their remarks. What other ways could you support being there for someone else's ideas?

(1.) _____

(2.) _____

(3.) _____

(4.) _____

(5.) _____

Listen. What messages emerge?

What other messages do I have about listening? Allow your higher self to speak. What guidance shows up? Write it here.

?

?

?

?

?

?

?

?

?

Write about being a good LISTENER.

Listening has been an integral part of crafting our own guidance. It is easier to listen to others' guidance. What about our own? What does our inner voice tell us? You might have to get really quiet and try over the course of several weeks or months. What stories do you tell about yourself? First and foremost, are they true? Are they kind? If not, then keep listening. You will uncover your true, essential guidance. Put it here once you find it.

_____

_____

_____

_____

_____

_____

_____

_____

_____

_____

_____

Draw what you hear.
What does
LISTENING look
like?

34 Maintain.

Who would have ever thought that maintaining status quo would ever be a good thing? However, it often is a wonderful thing. In the eye of the storm, you can find that calm place. Maintaining reminds me of the keel of the boat. Even when the boat tips over, the keel will always help the boat to bounce back to its upright position. To maintain grounding is to know consistency no matter what. To maintain is to continue, to carry on, and to keep going.

Maslow's hierarchy of needs is a concept presented in Abraham Maslow's theory of motivation paper in 1943 and later in his book, *Motivation and Personality* (1954). He believed essentially before you can pay attention to spiritual awakening, you must first make sure you have food, water, and shelter. There is more to his idea, but this is the essential gist. First things first. Has someone ever told you never make a big decision when you are hungry or tired?

"Sleep on it," they would say. This is central to the idea of maintaining.

Especially during hard times, just getting out of bed might be your win for today. Self-care will be key to keeping up or holding on. Get outside for a walk in nature as a great way to move through difficulty. Try to take things as objectively as possible, allowing things to roll off your back. This is hard when everyone is going through hardship at the same time. A dear friend often reminds me to be a non-emotional observer in my life. If I can step aside and just watch, I will be able maintain through an awkward situation.

Affirmation: I will stay the course. I will keep it moving. I will continue. I will hold on. I will make sure I have eaten, rested, and taken care of myself before making big decisions. I will find my center, ground, and let it all go.

Speak MAINTAIN into being.

What in your life would you like to keep, continue, or maintain? What would you like to let go? What no longer serves you?

(1.) _____

(2.) _____

(3.) _____

(4.) _____

(5.) _____

Listen. What messages emerge?

What does your non-emotional observer see? How can you detach from your experiences enough to release the emotional attachment of what happens to you? How can you maintain your peace amidst the storm? How can you let it go? How can you let it roll off your back?

?

?

?

?

?

?

?

Write about
MAINTAINING.

What basic needs of yours do you need to meet before you can focus on your spiritual awakening? What will help you stay the course? Do you have everything you desire? What is missing?

_____

_____

_____

_____

_____

_____

_____

_____

_____

_____

_____

_____

_____

_____

_____

_____

_____

_____

Draw MAINTAIN.
How do you stay the
course?

35 Motivate.

Over a decade ago, I went to an anger
management workshop. We all funneled into
the large conference room in the basement
of the office building. In the center of the
room was a large couch cushion and a
baseball bat. This is going to be great, I
thought.

One by one, we all took turns going to the
center of the room, picking up the bat and
hitting it against the cushion. Most of us
started out very gingerly. By the end, some
of us had bloody knuckles. Wrapped around
the cushion, you could hear us shouting,
"And another thing...!"

The role of the audience was the most
interesting of all. We were asked to cheer
on the person in the center of the room.
Each time, someone would begin, we would
urge them along. Now, when anger arises, I
allow it to flow through my body, and every
time I do, I hear the crowd cheering me
on. Releasing the shame that comes with

the emotion of anger, I can let it flow through me. Just like a storm, I can let it pass by.

I tell this story with this verb, because motivation requires your squad (internal or external) to cheer you along. To motivate requires stimulation, inspiration, enthusiasm, and interest. I think of the cheers, urging me to do something. This is what it feels like to be motivated. There is also a willingness to succeed and to maintain a consistent effort. Also included in motivation is getting rid of bad habits.

Affirmation: I will cheer myself on for staying the course! I will create a joy and an enthusiasm for what I am doing, how I am feeling, and my being-ness. I am willing to do my best! I am happy to call success to the forefront. I am inviting it in.

Speak about MOTIVATION.

If you were in the stands of the game of your life, how would you cheer yourself on? What would you be shouting to motivate yourself to score that goal?

(1.) _____

(2.) _____

(3.) _____

(4.) _____

(5.) _____

Listen. What messages emerge?

What do I already know about what motivates me? What other messages do I realize about motivation? How can I witness my own success, envision it before it happens? Every day is a new day! What if it were true that I could always start fresh?

?

?

?

?

?

?

?

Write about MOTIVATION.

What are some bad habits that I need to get rid of in order to become more effective? How can I focus on the donut and not the hole? How can I stop paying attention to the trivial stuff that distracts me from my purpose? What hard lessons or feelings have I been avoiding?

_____

_____

_____

_____

_____

_____

_____

_____

_____

_____

_____

_____

_____

_____

_____

Draw your greatest
MOTIVATORS.

36 Nurture.

How many of us nurture ourselves? We are all so great at nurturing others, especially as parents. We are usually the last to receive our own love and care. What would it feel like if we could turn all the love and nurture we send out to others back onto ourselves?

This action is about self-nurture. This means really being there for yourself no matter what. If you are sad, angry, even happy or elated, do you shut down when you are feeling your emotions? Where do you go? What do you do? Love and respect the person you are. Allow yourself to experience your feelings. Be there for yourself. Show up for yourself. Give yourself the nurturing feedback that you would give to someone who is not feeling their best. What would that sound like? What would that look like? It is easier to nurture a loved one, even a close confident or co-worker, than to nurure yourself. Watch how you love and care for them. Then try these same techniques on yourself. Oftentimes, we give away the care we desperately need to receive ourselves.

Mirror Practice:

(1.) Share your thoughts, feelings, etc.

(2.) Looking into a mirror, affirm what you just said/heard.

Affirmation: I love you. You are safe to feel whatever it is you are feeling. You are safe to say what you need to say. I am here to listen to you, no matter what. It is safe for you to voice your needs. I will help you get your needs met. You are appreciated. You are important. You are loved.

Speak NURTURING into being.

Allow the questions to come. What will it take for you to nurture yourself? Ask five (or more) questions that you ask about loving and caring for yourself.

(1.) _____

(2.) _____

(3.) _____

(4.) _____

(5.) _____

Listen. What messages emerge?

What other messages do I have about self-nurture? What are my next best right steps? Create a list of more verbs to help you move forward.

?

?

?

?

?

?

?

?

?

Write NURTURE down.

How do you feel about yourself? How do you comfort yourself? What do you do to care for yourself? I am sure you have heard it before. You cannot love someone else if you do not love yourself. Give yourself the opportunity to offer yourself deep care, just the way you would do for someone else. It feels good to be loved and cared for.

_____

_____

_____

_____

_____

_____

_____

_____

_____

_____

_____

_____

_____

Draw NURTURE.
How does it look?

37 Offer.

The verb "to offer" is synonymous with the word "to give." There are two scenarios below. Close your eyes Duh, you are reading. Ah well, maybe take a break after you read the next two passages! Imagine yourself in these situations.

(1.)   Situation 1: Imagine that you are on a crowded subway. You are sitting down and there are many people standing around you. Then, at the next stop, a very old passenger enters the train. You have an abled-body in this scenario and can very easily stand. You offer your seat to this passenger, who responds to you in gratitude.

(2.)   Situation 2: Say you go to a second hand bookstore with several books that you would like to sell for credit so you can buy new books to read. The clerk comes back with an offer. You either accept it or you do not. There is some value derived from what you are exchanging. You can decide if it is worth it or not.

Now, apply these two situations to yourself. Do you offer yourself a break when you are tired and ailing parts show up? Are other parts of you grateful when you do give yourself the gift of ease? What do you have to offer yourself (and others)? Do you find value and appreciate all you have to offer? Do you give your gifts freely? Do you see your own worthiness? Do you honor your own value?

Affirmation: I will gladly give myself a break when I have pushed too hard. I will also accept my gifts as value I can offer the world. I will pause at my wonder and worth and say "thank you." I will pause in gratitude for all I have to give the world. I will offer my gifts, free of attachments and expectations.

Speak OFFERING into being.

Allow the questions to come. What will it take for you see yourself as an offering, a blessing, a gift? Here are five (or more) questions that I ask about how I might give my gifts freely to the world.

(1.) _____

(2.) _____

(3.) _____

(4.) _____

(5.) _____

Listen. What messages emerge?

What other messages do I have about offering? What are my next best right steps?

Create a list of more verbs to help you give with gratitude.

?

?

?

?

?

?

?

?

Write about OFFERING.

Write down one thing that you will offer to someone else. It could be an object, time or a service. Allow yourself to give freely without expectations. Now, write down some things that you will offer to yourself. Write them down, schedule them, and do them! You will thank yourself for all you have to offer.

_____

_____

_____

_____

_____

_____

_____

_____

_____

_____

_____

_____

_____

_____

Draw OFFER. How
does it look?

38 Persevere.

To persevere means to continue along a course of action. This will be important when following "verbs as guidance". Often, you might look for the best next right step, and this is important. After you take each next right step, look for the next step and the step after that. Stay in the present moment. Actually remaining present is the crucial part.

I am reminded of the image of a staircase. If I stand at the bottom of the stairwell and peer upwards, getting to the top looks daunting. Just getting to the next step is how I will begin. Then I can take another step. Baby steps, one after another, will help me arrive at reaching the goal of climbing the stairs. Just start. And then, just continue. And then, start again. And then, continue again. Sometimes you will not be able to see the full staircase, and that is most definitely okay. Taking the next step in the best direction.

Let go of outcome. It will be important for you to let go of your expectations. When you allow yourself to lose sight of your destination, you will allow the energy to come into physical form in the way it was intended. Subconsciously, you might attach yourself to a defined outcome and set yourself up for the unobtainable. With perseverance, you remove your prospect of success and hold on. The divisional president of my old employer used to always say, "Bash on regardless." As it turns out, success usually shows up when you let go.

Affirmation: I will remain open. I will remind myself that I am never stuck. I always have choices and possibilities with every action. I will remain positive, grateful, and open. I am able to move to the next best right step.

Speak about PERSEVERING.

What are some immediate actions that I can take that will help me keep going? If I can write them down in a sequential order, very much like directions, then I can follow them later. What are some one-step-at-a-times that I can take immediately? Sometimes, starting at the end and backing your thinking up is an incredibly helpful way to see how to reach your finish line.

(1.) _____

(2.) _____

(3.) _____

(4.) _____

(5.) _____

Listen to the guidance.

Letting go and letting God. Yes. Perseverance comes when I let go and hold on at the same time. Relying on something greater than myself, trusting and letting go of outcome will help me maintain endurance to stay the course.

What messages come in for you about staying aligned with your goals, hopes, and dreams?

?

?

?

?

?

?

Write it down. What does it mean?

What is one thing that you have held tightly because you so deeply believed in it? You did not give up, because you knew it would fully manifest and become something remarkable? If you have not had this experience yet, what would it look like? Allow yourself to dream a little.

_____

_____

_____

_____

_____

_____

_____

_____

_____

_____

_____

_____

_____

_____

_____

_____

Draw your
PERSEVERENCE.

39 Pivot.

We have done a lot of pivoting during the year of the global pandemic. Essentially, pivoting happens a lot in the game of basketball. With one foot firmly planted on the court, the basketball player picks up their other foot and rotates. This is a defensive move, protecting the basketball from the opposition. The player can pivot forever.

The official definition of pivot reminds us that a core remains essential to our lives. It stays fixed no matter what. Another thing rotates or moves around it, thereby allowing change to occur. This could very well be a nice analogy for divinity or God, as the central anchor in our lives. Everything else moves, or pivots, around our faith. It could also refer to our Higher Self and our lower-self. We are spiritual beings having human experiences.

To pivot means to maneuver. Maneuvering requires both skill and care. As we learn with the verb "to PRACTICE," both the skill and the care take great rehearsing. This care could mean care for others or engaging in self-care. Developing skills happens over time. It might be helpful to develop a plan for both skill development and caring for others.

Pivoting involves reinventing yourself, in turning away from rigidity to a fresh beginning. What new skills would you like to learn? Find the experts. Find a mentor. Learn from the best. Be easy on yourself by setting realistic goals. In the process, you may find new ways of thinking, building confidence, and increasing your cooperation and collaboration with your teams or families.

Affirmation: I will learn new ways of caring and new skillsets in order to maneuver differently in my life. I can pivot many times in my life, until I feel safe or until I "get it right." I will decide what is central in my life, whether it is God, or my Higher Self, and revolve my life around that. I will work continually to reinvent myself.

Speak about PIVOTING.

What are some central, core elements in my life that I would like to anchor or ground? What is essential? What must remain fixed that is non-negotiable? What role does my faith play in creating a centralized anchor in my life?

(1.) _____

(2.) _____

(3.) _____

(4.) _____

(5.) _____

Listen to the guidance of the PIVOT.

What are my next moves? As I pivot, how do I wish to reinvent myself?

Create a list of skills you would like to develop.

?

?

?

?

?

?

?

Write it down.

You have learned how to stay present during a time of uncertainty. Look at what you would like to keep in your life and examine what you would like to discard. This examination will help you get clear on how you might wish to pivot, whether a slight turn, a 180° direction change, or coming full circle, all 360°. Wish it into being!

_____

_____

_____

_____

_____

_____

_____

_____

_____

_____

_____

_____

_____

_____

_____

_____

_____

_____

Draw the PIVOT.

40 Practice.

Absolutely EVERYTHING takes practice.
Have you ever watched the most brilliant
musicians play their instruments with
magnificent skill? Do you think they always
sounded like that? I assure you they did
not. Their tenacious persistence paid off,
allowing them to become great.

Positive thinking also takes practice.
Conversely, so does toxic negativity! You
have to decide which you want, and then
persevere or persist to become really
accomplished. All to say, it is a choice! You
can practice thinking the thoughts you
would like. You get to decide.

(1.)   Make a vow. For example, "I vow
       to watch my thinking and my
       words for 30 days." Or, perhaps
       you will say, "I promise to treat
       people kindly."

(2.)   Try something new. It is
       exhilarating to start doing

something that you have never done. It is challenging at the beginning, but it is so gratifying when you start getting the hang of it. For example, I started learning French. After practicing grammar exercises and learning the form, it is exhilarating to enter into a conversation with someone and be understood!

(3.) Do not quit. We all have a tendency to give up when something does not come easily or right away. Stick with it. Imagine that your breakthrough is right around the bend. Give it one more shot.

Practice makes progress. There is no such thing as perfection. You will never reach it. Progress, on the other hand, is very much possible. As you advocate for yourself, encourage yourself to step out of your comfort zone, and progress will be yours!

Affirmation: I will give myself a chance to experience progress and breakthroughs.

Speak your PRACTICE into being.

What are some of my intensions? How would my inner-leader like to practice? What would I like to improve? What would I like to make "scary good" in my life? What do I see that you know needs improvement? Where can you add a little persistence and tenacity to see what shows up?

(1.) _____

(2.) _____

(3.) _____

(4.) _____

(5.) _____

Listen. What messages emerge?

Allow the questions to come. What would I like to improve? What more would I like to learn?

How you might you like to spend your time and energy?

?

?

?

?

?

?

?

?

Write about PRACTICE.

Write about your spiritual practice. What does it look like now? How would you like it to look? What activities would you like to do each day to experience progress?

_____

_____

_____

_____

_____

_____

_____

_____

_____

_____

_____

_____

_____

_____

_____

_____

_____

_____

Draw your
PRACTICE.

41 Realize.

To realize is to become fully aware, to understand clearly. It also might mean that you have caused something to happen. It might be connected with manifesting. How does one increase awareness? Here are some strategies:

(1.) The biggest, best advice is to slow down and notice. Look around and really look. What do you see? What do you hear? What do you smell? Feel?

(2.) Long, slow breathing exercises might help you slow down, as would meditation. Start by taking a long breath in through your nose and letting it out quickly through your mouth. Do it again but slow down the breathing.

(3.) If your computer brain is swirling, either journal your thoughts or write a list of all the things you need to do. These two practices will empty your mind and allow you to settle. Once you settle into your surroundings, you will be able to open to awareness and realization of deepening.

Awareness comes in its external and internal forms. Realizing is about getting to know your inner being. Realizing means becoming the best version of yourself.

Realize your true potential. Realize your destiny. As the co-creator of your life, you hold great power in determining what happens in your life, or at the very least, how you react to it. May you recognize your own brilliance and beauty. May you allow yourself to recognize your powerful potential.

Affirmation: I am much wiser than I know. I am much smarter than I ever thought I could be. I am more beautiful than I could observe in the mirror. I will realize my greatest potential and dreams by starting with me and my most immediate peers.

Speak REALIZE into being.

What are some things you observe? When you slow your vibration down, and even out your breathing, what do you notice around you? What do you notice within? What do you recognize about your greatness?

(1.) _____

(2.) _____

(3.) _____

(4.) _____

(5.) _____

Listen. What messages emerge?

Allow the questions to come. Allow my higher power tell me who I really am, so that I will be able to recognize my own brilliance when I see it.

?

?

?

?

?

?

?

?

?

Write about
REALIZE.

What are some things you realize? What now makes sense? What are some of your deepest aha moments?

_____

_____

_____

_____

_____

_____

_____

_____

_____

_____

_____

_____

_____

_____

_____

_____

_____

_____

_____

Draw what you would like to REALIZE.

42 Recognize.

Recognizing is about being able to tell the difference between your false ego-selves and your own true Spirit or nature. To recognize implies that you have seen something before, only to know it once again. Because we come from Source, we will know it when we see it. To see our Source once more, found within our true nature, we recognize our true selves.

It is our greatest quest to recognize our truest selves and greet them when they appear. "There you are," you will say. "I've been waiting for you." You will welcome your truest selves in and have them join you in the sitting room. You will talk to them for awhile and get to know them. They will stay awhile, and you will authentically feel yourself, in all your full radiance.

Part of recognizing something is also acknowledging, or validating, it. Recognition works really well if you can work to validate yourself, acknowledge your beautiful nature, and give thanks for being exactly as you are. All too often, we are very good at acknowledging the beauty or wisdom of others, and we forget to extend this to ourselves. The practice of seeing others as your mirror is a spectacular exercise. When you see beauty in someone else, you might recognize it as your experience of their beauty, or a mirror of your own beauty. This works conversely with ugliness, too. When you see something that displeases you, perhaps it is a wake-up call for you to work on recognizing your own thoughts, as they are within yourself.

Affirmation: My dear true self, I will feel safe and comfortable to openly show myself to myself. I see you in me. May I recognize my true self today. May I grow in love and recognize how far I have come. I recognize myself as the infinite being that I am. I will see my divinity in others, as well as within myself. I will appreciate this recognition wherever I see it.

Speak RECOGNITION into being.

Allow the questions to come. How will I validate myself? How will I acknowledge my own loveliness today? Here are five (or more) questions that I ask about really seeing myself as I am...and knowing me for the very first time.

(1.) _____

(2.) _____

(3.) _____

(4.) _____

(5.) _____

Listen. what messages emerge?

Let my Higher Self, also known as my Source speak. what would I say if my ego-self did not try to dominate the conversation?

write the messages here.

?

?

?

?

?

?

?

?

Write about RECOGNITION.

"If you spot it, you've got it!" is a great reminder that we all are working on ourselves. Casting judgement elsewhere eliminates the possibility of our finding our own solutions. Recognizing our wondrous nature and our shadow side will help us to reach wholeness and to recognize that we are in a continual space of healing and growing.

Write down some of the things you recognize about yourself that you also see in others.

_____

_____

_____

_____

_____

_____

_____

_____

Draw yourself. What do you RECOGNIZE?

43 Reflect.

Reflecting is about taking the time to process. Reflecting is literally holding up a mirror so you can see what is there and allowing for a response to it. Reflecting is a very open-ended and open-minded activity that includes meta-cognition (thinking about your thinking). Reflecting is not analyzing, judging, or critiquing. How have you changed over the years? What lessons have you learned?

In our harried lives, it is hard to find time to sit back and observe, process, and understand. So often, we do not. Sometimes, it takes the act of setting parameters around our time, so that we can spend time in reflection. Put time to reflect on your calendar in order to think deeply and carefully.

Explore this: Go to the mirror and sit in front of it. Sit and write, observe, and ask questions aloud to yourself. What do you see? What are you surprised to see? Look deeply into your own eyes. Who is this person in front of you? Say to yourself, "I love you."

Built into reflecting is deep listening, both to yourself and to others. A reflective listening practice is to be able to repeat what you just heard. You will be surprised at how much work this skill requires. Sit with another person and work with each other until you can accurately reflect aloud what you hear. Validation and respect are direct results of this practice. Trust also increases because you become a better listener.

Affirmation: I am a reflection of my beautiful spirit within. I am not my ego. I am not my work. I am personified divinity. I am light. I am a reflection of my wholeness within. I will listen to others and myself today. I will really hear what is being said. I will work until I see significant progress. I am safe to make mistakes. I am safe to try again. I will carve out time for deep thinking and processing time.

Speak REFLECTING into being.

Allow the questions to come. What will I reflect on today? Here are five (or more) questions that I ask about really seeing myself as I am.

(1.) _____

(2.) _____

(3.) _____

(4.) _____

(5.) _____

Listen. What do you hear?

What other messages do I hold about self-reflection? What are my next best right steps?

Create a list of more verbs to help find your true self within.

?

?

?

?

?

?

?

?

Write about
REFLECTING.

Take this moment to reflect upon your day, your week, your year, and your life. Consider your past, your present, and your future. Where are you? Where do you see yourself? More importantly, how are you?

_____

_____

_____

_____

_____

_____

_____

_____

_____

_____

_____

_____

_____

_____

_____

_____

_____

_____

Draw your own
REFLECTION. what
shows up?

44 Remember.

The act of remembering is often associated with recalling information that has been memorized formally. The kind of remembering that is important here is about bringing to your mind an awareness of your own greatness.

Remember who you are. We are born into this world with perfect knowledge of who we are. Then, we look to the people around us to help us fit into the world as babies, children, teenagers, and adults. Very rarely do we remember who we are. Relying on external sources for validation and confirmation, we slip into a hazy recognition of who we first knew ourselves to be.

I remember hearing on the internet about a girl who had been bullied at school. Her mom said to her, "Don't forget who you are and whose you are." It will be important for you to go within and sit quietly. In order to remember who you truly are, you must quiet the inner dialogue (and the external dialogue, too). You must sit and listen. Wait for the remembrances to come. They might not come right away. Allow your ego to sit this one out. Your spirit, or your higher power, will help you remember exactly who you are. Take a deep breath and listen for the answer.

Affirmation: I am committed to remembering who I am. I am a child of the universe, a child of God. I am a spiritual being having a human experience. I am whole. I am perfect just the way I am. I am a marvelous creation. I am needed here to do my life's work. I know exactly who I am. I am smart. I am beautiful. I am doing the very best and worst that I can with what I have available to me.

REMEMBER your true self.

What would I like to remember? What would I like my inner being to explain to me? What is important for me to realize in this moment?

(1.) _____

(2.) _____

(3.) _____

(4.) _____

(5.) _____

Listen. What messages emerge?

What other messages do I receive about remembering my truest nature? What are my next best right steps? Ask your deepest, most sincerest questions here. Then, spend some time writing the answers down. You will be amazed. They will come. With practice, you will be able to offer your own guidance, recall memories, and look into the future. Begin right now. Do not overthink it.

?

?

?

?

?

?

Write about
REMEMBERING.

Write down a few memories that you have from your childhood. Try to write what you thought about and the dreams you had for yourself at that time. Are they still present with you, or did they go to sleep in your attempt to "adult" and hold it all together, as you thought you must?

_____

_____

_____

_____

_____

_____

_____

_____

_____

_____

_____

_____

_____

_____

_____

_____

Draw what it means
to REMEMBER.
Draw your true self
into being. Your
muscle memory
remembers. Allow
yourself be guided.
Draw whatever
emerges.

45 Reside.

There are two big ideas that come with the action of residing:

(1.)   Belonging

(2.)   Feeling at home

To reside means that you are habitually present, that you keep coming back to the present moment, again and again. You return home. Belonging-ness and at-home-ness can both be experienced simiultaneously in the present moment. Reside right where you are, grounded.

The best place to reside is with yourself, where you can authentically be YOUniquely you, wherever your life experience has placed you. No matter what is happening in your physical experience, if you reside with your inner, real self, then you can find peace everywhere, within and without.

when you belong somewhere, or to

something, you are rightly placed in a specific position and have the qualities needed for the larger group. You might ask yourself, "Why am I here, doing what I'm doing?" There are no accidents, no coincidences. You have been placed right here for a very specific purpose.

Taking up residence somewhere, anchoring and establishing roots, could occur physically where you are, or could also mean residing mentally, emotionally, and spiritually. Feeling at home in your body, with who you are, brings about safety and stability. Consistency is a by-product of residence, which is the nucleus of good leadership.

Affirmation: I belong here. I am welcome here. I have permission to be here. I am safe to be who I am. I am welcome to be who I am. I am needed here. I am required here to bring my special gifts. I am part of a greater whole. I have the courage to be visible.

Speak RESIDENCE into being.

Allow the questions to come. What will it take for me to feel completely at home within myself? How do I feel when I belong? Here are five (or more) questions that I ask about loving and caring for myself.

(1.) _____

(2.) _____

(3.) _____

(4.) _____

(5.) _____

Listen. What messages emerge?

What other messages do I embrace about residing easily in my life? What are my next best right steps?

Create a list of more verbs to help you settle into your life comfortably.

?

?

?

?

?

?

?

?

Write about
RESIDING.

Take a look around you. Take a look within yourself. Where are you residing? Where have you put down your anchor? What mindset have you decided to settle into? What changes can you initiate? Do you choose to reside with peace and positivity, or have you gotten comfortable with hardship and negativity? It is your choice. Write down where you choose to reside today.

_____

_____

_____

_____

_____

_____

_____

_____

_____

_____

_____

_____

_____

Draw RESIDE. How does residency show up for you?

46 Rise.

To rise means to move from a lower
position to a higher one, as one would move
from sitting, to kneeling, to standing. This
quotation from Martin Luther King, Jr. is
relevant for this action word: "If you can't
fly then run. If you can't run then walk. If
you can't walk then crawl, but whatever
you do, you have to keep moving forward."
You are not expected to fly if you are in
crawl-mode or run if you are walking. Start
where you are and rise to the next occasion.
What is the next immediate activity? Bit
by bit, you will be able to fly, but it does not
have to happen immediately.

Rising up includes the idea of gradual
growth and improvement. Rising is about
doing things on purpose with the goal of
getting better at something. Just like the
length of daylight increases from winter
through springtime, add a few more
minutes onto your exercise practice, start
reading at bedtime for only five minutes,
and then gradually increase. This is meant

to be a gentle process. You may not immediately realize it, but as you step one foot in front of the other, you are actually growing and changing by leaps and bounds.

Rising also means emerging, just like the sun coming up from behind the horizon. Having the courage to be visible, allow yourself to stand up for something that you find important, or say what is needed to be said. Allow your true, authentic self to emerge from behind your ego. Listen to your spirit speak without your ego-filter. What is your best guidance? What is needed right now?

Affirmation: I will live on-purpose but with gentleness. I will take the next best right step towards growth and change. I will allow my true self to show itself as I welcome new growth and remove my façade. I will start right where I am without immediately trying to do too much in the process. I will give myself ease and permission to rise to the occasion.

Speak RISING into being.

Allow the questions to come. What will I do purposefully to properly position myself for growth and gradual improvement? Here are five (or more) questions that I ask about loving and caring for myself.

(1.) _____

(2.) _____

(3.) _____

(4.) _____

(5.) _____

Listen. What messages emerge?

Without any sense of stress, and with full ease, what is the next best step that moves me in the direction that I would like to go?

What are my next best right steps? Create a list of more verbs to help you rise magnificently to the occasion.

?

?

?

?

?

?

?

Rise to the Occasion.

Moving and accomplishing with purpose means that you understand how each action fits into a larger vision. Rising up means being your own best guide. Do not censor yourself. Curb your desire to edit your words. Just get them onto paper. Ask yourself, "What is my larger vision? What is my personal mission statement?"

My Vision Statement (a larger guiding principle over the long-term):

_____

_____

_____

_____

_____

My Mission Statement (a summary of my specific purpose of being):

_____

_____

_____

_____

_____

Draw RISE. How does purpose look?

47 Seek.

As an official definition, the verb to SEEK
means to attempt to find something or to
ask for something. There are two key
components here: asking for what you want
and trying it out. The best part? You
cannot do this wrong, this life thing. It is
impossible. All of the opportunities that
come to you are for you. If they do not
come to you, then they were not meant for
you.

If you set an intention, the next part is to
allow. When you ask for something, you
might believe that you are just asking
allows it to come to fruition. What actually
happens is that you often end up
distracted, paying attention to something
else, the very thing you're focusing on,
whether it is fear, anxiety, worry, or anger,
will come into being instead. Ask and allow.
Seeking fuels this allowance. Go ahead and
move your fearful or hesitant self out of
your own opening way.

"Ask, and it shall be given to you; seek, and ye shall find; knock, and it shall be opened unto you" (Bible, Matthew 7:7-8). Have you ever been thinking about something, only to then see or hear what you desire everywhere? Make sure you are seeking what you really want. If you are dissatisfied by what appears, check yourself. As your life's co-creator, you are responsible for what comes in and what goes out. You have the opportunity to change the trajectory and seek something else. Everything is workable, and you always have daily decisions to make. You are never stuck. Look beyond the immediate situation and expand the conversation. Sometimes, the view is too narrow. Open it up and see what happens.

Affirmation: I am available for the abundance I seek. I am open to the success that I desire. I am fulfilled, happy, and whole. I will ask for what I want. I will allow it to come into my experience. I will appreciate the process. I will make sure to look around and within myself. I will give the search my best go.

Speak about being a SEEKER.

Make a wish list of things you are curious about, or things you would like to have in your life that currently are not manifested. Would you like to be working on something that has not emerged yet? Why or why not?

(1.) _____

(2.) _____

(3.) _____

(4.) _____

(5.) _____

Listen. What messages emerge?

Allow your inner self to speak to you. What do I seek? What do I search for? What am I looking for? What do I desire? The inner-guidance will emerge.

?

?

?

?

?

?

?

?

?

Write about what you SEEK.

Write about your intentions and desires, as well as all the things that you keep in your mental "Someday-Maybe" folder. What is it that you desire and require out of life? Ask for these things, and allow them to come into your experience.

_____
_____
_____
_____
_____
_____
_____
_____
_____
_____
_____
_____
_____
_____
_____
_____

Draw what you are
SEEKING.

48 Serve.

Perhaps you have heard of the concept of the "Servant Leader," coined from an essay written by Robert K. Greenleaf in 1970. Since then, this concept has grown into a movement unto itself. The original concept, however, was very simple: be a servant first before assuming your role as CEO, administrative assistant, VP, or project manager, etc. By focusing on the needs of others around you, especially those on your team, you place your own needs as secondary to theirs. The Biblical Golden Rule, doing for others, as you would like others to do for you, is à propos to this concept.

In several Eastern religions, such as Hinduism, Buddhism, and Jainism, there is a spiritual concept called *Seva*, which is a Sanskrit word that means selfless service. It is one of the most important spiritual concepts you will find in many yoga practices. For example, it is present in karma yoga, or the practice of selfless action, where you are asked to serve others with no expectation of an outcome. It is the practice of having an interest in the well-being of others, a deep expression of compassion, and a real desire to lift the spirits of those around you. Serving others is a devotional practice that is an indirect way of serving God, or your Higher Power.

Affirmation: I will serve my divine source and others around me with gladness. I will come into God's presence with singing (Psalm 100). I will do things for others with gratitude for each opportunity to serve. I will invest in the care of others and while not forgetting about my own self-care. I will let go of expecting an outcome as I do things for others. I serve with compassion. I will examine my own expectations that I place on others as I do favors for them. I will selflessly give of my time and energy to make someone's day better, or to help a project go more smoothly.

Speak SEVA (selfless service) into being.

Allow the questions to come. What will it take to do more for others? Here are five (or more) questions that I also ask about loving and caring for myself.

(1.) _____

(2.) _____

(3.) _____

(4.) _____

(5.) _____

Listen. What messages emerge?

What other messages that come about serving others? What are my next best right steps to bring the spiritual practice of selfless service into my life?

Create a list of more verbs to help you let go of outcome.

?

?

?

?

?

?

?

Write about selfless SERVICE.

It is possible to imagine this action in two ways: performing tasks for others or serving something to someone at a table. In both of these cases, how are the tasks being performed? Selflessly? With strings attached? What are you serving to them for dinner? Is it a delicious meal cooked with love, or are you sharing negativity in the form of burned leftovers? The choice is yours.

_____

_____

_____

_____

_____

_____

_____

_____

_____

_____

_____

_____

_____

Draw SERVING others. How does doing for others make you feel?

49 Shift.

Shift happens. We have all gone through some sort of shift, a metamorphosis of sorts. An enormous paradigm shift has occurred as a result of the global pandemic. And, as much as we wouldn't like to admit a major change, here we are. I think of a caterpillar's journey in becoming a butterfly. Everything must completely come apart for it to transform fundamentally. The results can be exquisite and exceptionally beautiful. I imagine a phoenix rising from the ashes. We will rebuild, piece by piece.

The more we are required to change, the more we are required to stay put. As you learn to offer your own guidance amidst this massive shift, learn too to stay put as a way to explore your own life. If something comes up that hurts, if something does not feel good, do not shut down. Stay put and be right where you are. Imagining a rainstorm, what do you do? Either you wait for it to blow over, or you put on your raincoat, go out, and play in the puddles.

Either alternative or choice is a great response to the unexpected!

The paradox of shifting requires a simultaneous rootedness. Practice observing your own life shifting, as a key witness, and be the main protagonist at the same time. Observe this from a place of grounding. What do you notice when your emotions rise up? What do you do with these feelings and emotions? Do you hold onto them and let them soak in? Notice whether you respond with a fight-or-flight response when things get rough. Do you freeze? Do you put up your dukes and show your teeth? Do you don your mask and pretend? Stick with it as the world shifts around you. It is a good time to watch what you do.

Affirmation: I will relax into the change around me and work on staying in the present moment. I am safe to settle into any paradigm shift. I am courageous to be myself, even as things change around me. I am worthy of abundance. I am capable of changing and morphing into something new and beautiful. I will allow shift to happen.

Speak your SHIFT into being.

Allow the questions to come. What will it take for you to feel comfortable with change? How do I process transformation? Here are five (or more) questions that I ask when dealing with change.

(1.) _____

(2.) _____

(3.) _____

(4.) _____

(5.) _____

Listen. What messages emerge?

What other messages do I understand about my current paradigm shift? What are my next best right steps?

Create a list of additional verbs to help you stay put as you simultaneously practice metamorphosis. How are you like a caterpillar changing into a butterfly?

?

?

?

?

?

?

?

Write about the SHIFT.

When something unexpected or surprising comes up, stay with what is in the present moment. Let your responses be what they are. Write them down here, so you can see yourself in action. Commit to not leaving a challenging situation until you have a clear strategy, but allow yourself to transform. What does this transformation feel like? Write it here.

_____

_____

_____

_____

_____

_____

_____

_____

_____

_____

_____

_____

_____

Draw SHIFTING in action.

50 Transcend.

To transcend means to "rise above." It also means to go beyond the limits of something. This action can be mastered in two unique ways: rising above drama and achieving excellence.

To transcend a negative situation (external) or mindset (internal)—and it is all internal—you must remember that you cannot get where you want to go from where you are. In order to transcend a scenario, you must first change your mindset and attitude in order to adjust to the place you would like to be. This can be a physical location or a theoretical place of positivity. You could desire a drama-free zone at work. This requires transcendence, a not-buying-in, a not-taking-the-bait, a misery-does-NOT-love-company, an I-will-not-participate vantage point.

In order to transcend, in order to achieve excellence, one must hyperextend beyond the status quo. This takes extra energy and is not sustainable over the long haul. That is why transcendence of this depth must be used in conjunction with other actions like UNPLUG or UNWIND in order to recharge.

Lasting transcendence requires a "going-beyond." This transcendence will require tenacity and perseverance, even if you cannot see the end from where you are. It will require trust that you will get there. Both come about from an attitude of gratitude. Having the courage to be grateful will afford transcendence in both fostering positivity and facilitating excellence.

Affirmation: I am grateful to be doing abc with xyz. I am thankful for the opportunity to share my expertise and skillset. I will model different behavior, at all costs. I will model the change I want to see. As Ghandi said, "Be the change you wish to see in the world."

Speak TRANSCENDENCE into being.

Allow the questions to come. What will it take to transcend your current situation? Here are five (or more) questions that I ask about "rising above" and achieving excellence.

(1.) _____

(2.) _____

(3.) _____

(4.) _____

(5.) _____

What other messages do I have for myself about transcendence?

What are my next best right steps? Create a list of more verbs to help you move forward.

?

?

?

?

?

?

?

Write about
TRANSCENDING.

Write down one action that you will take today or this week that will really allow you to shift your attitude, change your mindset, or be successful beyond your original expectations (or wildest dreams). Write it down, schedule it, and do it. Your mind, body, and spirit will thank you. Be sure to include a way to refresh yourself afterwards.

_____

_____

_____

_____

_____

_____

_____

_____

_____

_____

_____

_____

_____

Draw TRANSCEND.
How does it look?

51 Unplug.

To unplug means to turn oneself off. Power down. REST. STOP. Unplugging is critical for maximum engagement when you are on, or leading, or let's face it, while at work or with your family. Do you really know where your off switch is? When you "unplug," do you stay off?

Maybe you are nodding "yes," but then you lie down with your laptop open or you are plugged into your phone while spending time with your family. Sound familiar? Why are you using _ON-NESS_ and _BUSY-NESS_ as a distraction? Why are you numbing out? What are you hiding from? Stay present. Don't overdo it. Easy does it. There is no medal for running yourself into the ground. Self-care is as critical as is caring for your team. You cannot do one without the other. Both are necessary.

It is critical to shut down every night before you go to sleep and spend at least one day during the weekend doing nothing, or at the bare minimum, doing something that allows you to recharge. We let our phones recharge, but we do not afford ourselves the same luxury. Why is that? Try setting an alarm to rest. Try putting rest on your "to-do" list.

Two themes:

    (1.)   Attend to the task at hand.

    (2.) Stop doing.

Affirmation: I am safe to let go. I am important in my own life. I allow myself to rest. I am safe to unplug.

Speak UNPLUG into being.

Allow the questions to come. What will it take to unplug? Here are five (or more) questions that I wonder about.

(1.) _____

(2.) _____

(3.) _____

(4.) _____

(5.) _____

Listen. What messages emerge?

What other messages do I notice for myself about unplugging? What are my next best right steps?

Create a list of more verbs to help you move forward.

?

?

?

?

?

?

?

?

Write about
UNPLUGGING.

Write down one action that you will take today or this week that will genuinely allow you to pause, shut down, and unplug. Write it down, schedule it, and do it. Your mind, body, and spirit will thank you. (By the way, sleep is an acceptable activity.)

_____

_____

_____

_____

_____

_____

_____

_____

_____

_____

_____

_____

_____

_____

_____

Draw UNPLUG. What does it look like?

52 Unwind.

Unwinding is similar to unplugging. Also crucial for stress relief, it is a deep "letting go." To unwind is a form of release. It is an undoing, an unraveling.

Imagine that you are sitting on a swing at your childhood playground. Try to remember if you used to twist the chains together. Winding and rotating, the chains would become completely twisted. As you work, you twist, and you twist, and you twist, until you cannot do it anymore. Many of us do not lift up our feet to let the twisted chains unwind. This is the next best step. Lift up your feet and feel the dizziness of unwinding come over you when the chains loosen and finally become separate again, most likely, you will feel joy as a result!

After each workday, remember to pick up your feet and allow yourself to come back to center. Tomorrow, you can begin to twist again. For now, give yourself permission to let go. How can I remember to pick up my feet? What actions can I build into my day to ensure that I create time to unwind?

(1.)   Pick up feet.
(2.)   Hold onto the chains.
(3.)   Throw your head back.
(4.)   Kick out your feet in front of you.
(5.)   Smile.

Affirmation: I will allow unwinding to be a joyful experience. I am happy to be unwinding. I am safe to unwind. I am allowed to unwind. Unwinding brings joy to my life.

Speak about UNWINDING.

Allow the questions to come. What will it take to unwind? Here are five (or more) questions that I wonder about.

(1.) _____

(2.) _____

(3.) _____

(4.) _____

(5.) _____

Listen to the guidance of UNWINDING.

What are my next best right steps? As I unwind, what do I hear from my inner guidance? What are my next best right steps?

Create a list of more verbs to help you move forward.

?

?

?

?

?

?

Write it down.

What is one thing that you will do that will allow yourself to unwind and come back to center? Whether you are into exercise, meditation, or playing with your children, give yourself permission to do only that, so that you can come back to center and start fresh tomorrow.

_____

_____

_____

_____

_____

_____

_____

_____

_____

_____

_____

_____

_____

_____

_____

_____

_____

Draw it.

Closing Remarks on Being-ness. And, no, it isn't a verb!

After working with these fifty-two verbs, you might feel a little more grounded in your body. Your soul may have stretched out a little bit. You may start to feel more present in your life, a little more accountable. You may take a little more responsibility for your actions, thoughts, and the way you feel. You may start to notice things around you that you never have noticed before. On your way to work, as you go about getting ready for your day, and as you close down for the night, you might find yourself saying, "thank you" a little more often.

Being-ness does not require that you do anything special. Being-ness means that you notice where you are, what you are doing, and that do so with a brand new freshness. Your being-ness is your essence and your presence. You do not have to do anything special to create this, or to make it work. Simply experience it. It's right now. It is the present moment everybody always talks about. Someone said to me, "We are human *beings*, not human *doings*."

We are very good at shrouding our being-ness with our busy-ness and our doing-ness. We numb out by working, eating, drinking, sexting, thinking, or judging. Name your crutch. We all have one (or two...or three). No judgement whatsoever here! This work, creating your own guidance, is about uncovering our being-ness and falling in love with it, and who we are, one-step at a time.

If we can pause, breathe, and notice, then we can understand our lives and allow our inner guidance to reveal itself. We need it now more than ever. Ask yourself, "Are you riding or driving?" Sometimes, it can be helpful to take a ride in the passenger seat. See how much more you notice when you loosen your grip, give up control, or go along for the ride. It is an incredible practice. Let go. No, really. Put down your heaviness.

Take some time to go back and reread what you have written. Revisit these responses several weeks from now and write again. Compare your answers. Take a look at what you've drawn. Draw again after some time. Notice what has changed and what hasn't. You'll always be able to give yourself guidance in those places that need your wisdom and expertise. You can help parts of you that you would like to see shift. Finally, review your next best steps. Have you followed through with them? Notice your guidance. Notice what you listen to, what you require, desire, and deserve. What have you ignored? What needs your attention? Pull it forward. Practice makes progress.

As a leader, you will want to work on the connection between what you say and what you do. Do they match? If you can't ask yourself the hard questions, if you can't openly listen to your own truths, if you can't hold yourself accountable, then how can you expect those you lead to honor, trust, or respect you if you do not respect yourself?

Say often: "Practice makes progress." Life is not about achieving perfection, because you'll never get there. It doesn't exist. As a recovering perfectionist and workaholic, I can attest to this truth! Your distant goals for tomorrow will never be achieved today. Focus on right now and be right where you are. Ask yourself, as my grandmother used to ask, "What is the best use of my time right now?" What can I do immediately to make a difference? What can I do in two minutes that I have been putting off? Whom do I need to tell that I'm struggling so they hold me accountable? The short-term and long-term initiatives will all show up as they are needed right here, right now. Feel empowered to ask for help. Help will appear once you voice it.

I certainly am grateful for you. Thank you for the time and attention you have given to yourself. What an absolute gift you are. Thank you. xo

Now for My Own Closing Remarks.

Goal Evaluation: How have I progressed since I have begun this work?

(1.) Did I conduct a full self-examination by reviewing all 52-action words in depth?

(2.) What other action words are needed for my own guidance besides the 52 given?

(3.) Have I consistently engaged in what I have committed to do?

Anything left undone or unsaid? Write it here. You can keep this "to-be" list with you and work presently on each item that you write down.

_____

_____

_____

_____

_____

My Final Intention:

_____

_____

_____

_____

_____

What verb would I like to immediately put into action?

_____

_____

_____

_____

_____

My Top 3 Next Best Steps: What supporting verbs are needed to help realize this intention?

(1.)

(2.)

(3.)

My Final Drawing.